D0348168

easy soups

easy soups

simple recipes for hearty meals in a bowl

RYLAND
PETERS
& SMALL

LONDON NEW YORK

Senior Designer Iona Hoyle
Editor Delphine Lawrance
Picture Research Emily Westlake
Production Toby Marshall
Art Director Leslie Harrington
Publishing Director Alison Starling

First published in Great Britain in 2010
by Ryland Peters & Small
20–21 Jockey's Fields
London WC1R 4BW
www.rylandpeters.com

10 9 8 7 6 5 4 3 2

Text © Fiona Beckett, Vatcharin
Bhumichitr, Celia Brooks Brown, Maxine
Clark, Ross Dobson, Clare Ferguson,
Liz Franklin, Manisha Gambir Harkins,
Tonia George, Rachael Anne Hill,
Jennifer Joyce, Caroline Marson, Louise
Pickford, Linda Tubby, Laura Washburn
and Ryland Peters & Small 2010

Design and photographs
© Ryland Peters & Small 2010

The authors' moral rights have been
asserted. All rights reserved. No part
of this publication may be reproduced,
stored in a retrieval system or
transmitted in any form or by any
means, electronic, mechanical,
photocopying or otherwise, without
the prior permission of the publisher.

ISBN 978 1 84975 044 8

A CIP record for this book is available
from the British Library.

Printed in China

Notes
• All spoon measurements are level
unless otherwise specified.

• Eggs are medium unless otherwise
specified. Uncooked or partly cooked
eggs should not be served to the
very young, the very old, those with
compromised immune systems or to
pregnant women.

contents

introduction

Soup is one of those instantly satisfying, all-purpose dishes that fits any occasion, from a dinner party to a quick after-work meal for one. It's also a great way of using up any vegetables that you have to hand. Forget canned soups with their artificial flavourings, instead make your own from scratch and in no time at all.

The **Vegetables** section is bursting with traditional recipes such as tasty Gazpacho, Leek and Potato or Cauliflower and Stilton, as well as more unusual combinations. Try making the Celeriac and Orange soup or the Mushroom soup with Madeira.

A soup packed with **Pulses** is perfect for a wintry night in and more substantial too. The spicy Andalusian Chickpea soup is full of warming flavours while Lentil, Coconut and Wilted Spinach makes an ideal comforting dish. For something lighter but still high in flavour, try the Swiss Chard and White Bean broth or Flag Bean soup.

In **Meat and Poultry**, you will find some great recipes for serving everyday such as Sweetcorn and Chicken soup or hearty Harrira with lamb. Lighter soups include Chilled Melon soup with Serrano Ham or child-pleasing Alphabet soup. **Fish and Seafood** takes you from the Mediterranean all the way to the East, with recipes such as Spanish Bouillabaisse and Hot and Sour prawn soup.

With more than 120 recipes, inspired by cooking styles from around the world, *Easy Soups* is brimming with ideas for you to try.

vegetables

This classic summer soup hailing from Spain has dozens of variations, depending on its region of origin. The most essential ingredients however are sweet-smelling tomatoes to give the gazpacho the required strength of flavour.

gazpacho

30 g stale white bread, crusts removed

¼ red onion, chopped

3 garlic cloves, crushed

1 kg ripe tomatoes, quartered

1 red pepper, chopped

¼ cucumber, finely chopped

3 tablespoons sherry vinegar

100 ml extra virgin olive oil

a few drops of Tabasco

salt and black pepper

serves 6

Put the bread in a food processor and blend until you have crumbs, then tip into a bowl and set aside.

Fix the bowl back on the processor, add the onion and garlic and blend until chopped. Add the tomatoes and pepper and blend until puréed. Tip out and stir in the remaining ingredients and the breadcrumbs, adding a little water if it is too thick. Season generously and refrigerate for 2 hours.

Serve ice cold in shot glasses.

You won't be able to eat a huge amount of this soup as it is very rich and you can have too much of a good thing. The only stipulation here is that the avocados must be ripe or you won't get that nutty, creamy flavour they are so admired for.

chilled avocado soup

2 tablespoons avocado oil or extra virgin olive oil, plus extra to serve

2 garlic cloves, crushed

1 red chilli, deseeded and chopped

½ teaspoon ground cumin

4 spring onions, chopped

2 large tomatoes, skinned, deseeded and chopped

2 ripe avocados, halved and stoned

4 tablespoons Greek yoghurt

700 ml chilled vegetable or chicken stock

juice of 3 limes

10 g fresh coriander leaves

salt and black pepper

serves 4–6

Put the oil, garlic, chilli, cumin and spring onions in a frying pan over medium heat and cook for 1 minute. Add the tomatoes and cook for 3–4 minutes until you have a thick paste, then leave to cool slightly.

Transfer the contents of the frying pan to a blender and whizz with a pinch of salt until finely chopped. Scoop out the flesh of the avocados and add to the blender along with the yoghurt. Liquidize until smooth. Add the vegetable stock, lime juice and coriander and liquidize again. Season to taste.

Divide the soup between 4–6 bowls and drizzle with a little extra oil.

This soup contains a surprise – the layer of crème fraîche underneath the beetroot soup is invisible until you put your spoon in (and it also helps hold up the cucumber).

iced beetroot soup
with crème fraîche

500 g cooked beetroot, chopped

750 ml chicken or beef stock

1 tablespoon harissa paste,
or to taste

salt and black pepper

to serve

1 mini (Lebanese) cucumber or
about 10 cm regular cucumber

250 ml crème fraîche

ice cubes (optional)

freshly grated lemon zest or
4 teaspoons caviar (optional)

iced vodka

serves 4

Put the beetroot in a blender, add 2 ladles of stock and purée until smooth. Add the remaining stock and purée again. Test for thickness, then add the harissa paste and salt and pepper to taste, adding extra stock or water if the purée is too thick. Blend again, then chill very well. Chill all the remaining ingredients and your serving bowls.

To prepare the cucumber, cut off the ends and slice thinly on a mandoline or with a vegetable peeler. Cut it diagonally, or into rounds, or in cubes, as you like. If you are using a regular cucumber, cut the slices in quarters.

When ready to serve, put a layer of crème fraîche in each chilled serving bowl and spread it flat with the back of a spoon. Carefully pour the beetroot soup over the back of another spoon so it doesn't disturb the cream. Add a few ice cubes to each serving if you like. Put a few pieces of cucumber in the middle – the cream will hold them up – then sprinkle with a very little amount of finely grated lemon zest, if using. Serve with a shot of iced vodka.

This lighter version of an Italian classic makes a pleasing summer dish. It has added sparkle thanks to the last-minute addition of pesto and is ready to serve in under 20 minutes, leaving you maximum time to relax outside rather than being tied to the kitchen.

summer minestrone

50 g small dried pasta shapes, such as anellini or fedelini

1 tablespoon olive oil

1 red onion, chopped

1 garlic clove, finely chopped

2 celery sticks, thinly sliced

150 g baby carrots, thinly sliced

2 plum tomatoes, coarsely chopped

1.25 litres vegetable stock

150 g runner beans, thinly sliced

2 tablespoons green pesto

salt and black pepper

1 tablespoon freshly grated Parmesan cheese, to serve

serves 4

Bring a large saucepan of water to the boil. Add a good pinch of salt, then the pasta, and cook until al dente, or according to the timings on the packet. Drain well.

Meanwhile, heat the oil in another large saucepan, add the onion and garlic and cook gently for 3 minutes. Add the celery and carrots and cook for a further 2 minutes. Add the tomatoes and cook for a further 2 minutes.

Add the stock and beans, bring to the boil, then reduce to a simmer for 5–10 minutes, until the vegetables are cooked and tender.

Add the drained pasta, stir in the pesto and add salt and pepper to taste. Divide between 4 bowls, sprinkle with Parmesan and serve.

If you prefer to make your own farro mixture, use whatever you have in your collection of dried peas, beans, lentils and grains. Spelt, the major grain in the mix, is a very ancient wheat, which is also used to make bread. Some people prefer barley or other grains.

minestra di farro

2–4 tablespoons olive oil

1 carrot, finely chopped

1 onion, chopped

1–2 garlic cloves, finely chopped

500 g farro mixture*

1 bay leaf

1 litre chicken or vegetable stock

salt and black pepper

to serve

1 tablespoon freshly grated Parmesan cheese

olive oil

serves 4

Heat the oil in a large saucepan, add the carrot and onion and cook slowly until softened but not browned. Add the garlic and cook until softened.

Add the farro mixture, bay leaf and stock and bring to the boil. Simmer slowly until done, about 30 minutes. Season with salt and pepper after 20 minutes.

Ladle into soup bowls, then serve with a bowl of Parmesan and some olive oil for drizzling.

*Note To make your own mixture, use 200 g farro (spelt) or pearl barley, 100 g yellow split peas, 100 g green split peas and 100 g baby white beans (fagiolini). Soak the baby beans overnight in cold water before using.

Buy your Parmesan in a big chunk and hang on to the rinds in an airtight container in the fridge. Not only will you feel a sense of satisfaction at having used every last morsel of your cheese, it will add wonderful depth of flavour and saltiness to your minestrone.

minestrone with Parmesan

4 tablespoons extra virgin olive oil, plus extra to serve

2 carrots, chopped

1 red onion, chopped

4 celery sticks, diced, leaves reserved

6 garlic cloves, finely chopped

2 tablespoons chopped fresh flat leaf parsley

2 teaspoons tomato purée

400 g canned plum tomatoes, chopped

1 litre chicken or vegetable stock

410 g canned borlotti beans, rinsed and drained

Parmesan cheese rind (optional)

150 g spring greens, shredded

100 g spaghetti, broken up

salt and black pepper

freshly grated Parmesan cheese, to serve

serves 4–6

Heat the oil in a large, heavy-based saucepan, then add the carrots, onion, celery and garlic. Cover and sweat very slowly over low heat, stirring occasionally, until thoroughly softened.

Add the parsley, tomato purée and tomatoes and cook for 5 minutes. Pour in the stock and borlotti beans and bring to the boil. If using a Parmesan rind, add this now. Once boiling, add the spring greens and simmer for 20 minutes.

Add the spaghetti and cook for 2–3 minutes less than the manufacturer's instructions suggest (by the time you have ladled it into bowls it will be perfectly cooked). Season to taste.

Divide the soup between 4–6 bowls and drizzle with extra olive oil. Serve with a bowl of grated Parmesan to sprinkle over the top.

This soup is incredibly quick to make and has a wonderful, fresh flavour, yet is made almost entirely from storecupboard ingredients. Enjoy a taste of summer all year round.

conchigliette soup with peas, artichokes & chilli

1 tablespoon olive oil

1 onion, finely chopped

2 garlic cloves, finely chopped

2 red chillies, thinly sliced into rings

4 slices smoked streaky bacon, finely chopped

1 teaspoon fresh marjoram or oregano

400 g canned artichoke hearts in water, drained and quartered

100 g frozen peas

1.25 litres chicken stock

75 g dried pasta shapes, such as conchigliette or gnocchetti

salt and black pepper

2 tablespoons freshly grated Parmesan cheese, to serve

serves 4

Heat the oil in a large saucepan, add the onion, garlic, chilli and bacon and cook for 4–5 minutes until golden.

Add the marjoram, artichokes and peas and stir-fry for 2 minutes. Add the stock, bring to the boil, then simmer for 10 minutes.

Meanwhile, bring another large saucepan of water to the boil. Add a good pinch of salt, then the pasta, and cook until al dente, or according to the timings on the packet.

Drain the pasta and add it to the soup. Divide between 4 bowls, sprinkle with Parmesan, then serve.

There's nothing quite like a huge bowl of thick, warming ribollita on a damp autumn evening. Ribollita means 'reboiled', and is made from whatever vegetables are around, but usually contain beans and the delicious Tuscan black winter cabbage, cavolo nero. Savoy cabbage makes a good alternative.

la ribollita

250 g dried cannellini beans

150 ml olive oil

1 onion, finely chopped

1 carrot, chopped

1 celery stick, chopped

2 leeks, finely chopped

4 garlic cloves, finely chopped, plus 1 extra, peeled, for rubbing

1 white cabbage, finely sliced

1 large potato, chopped

4 medium courgettes, chopped

400 ml tomato passata

2 sprigs each of fresh rosemary, thyme and sage

1 dried red chilli

500 g cavolo nero, finely sliced

6 thick slices crusty white bread

salt and black pepper

freshly grated Parmesan cheese, to serve

serves 8 generously

Put the beans in a bowl, cover with cold water, soak overnight, then drain just before you're ready to use them.

Next day, heat half the oil in a large, heavy-based saucepan and add the onion, carrot and celery. Cook gently for 10 minutes, stirring frequently. Add the leeks and garlic and cook for 10 minutes. Add the white cabbage, potato and courgettes, stir well and cook for 10 minutes, stirring frequently.

Stir in the soaked beans, passata, herbs, dried chilli, salt and plenty of black pepper. Cover with about 2 litres water (the vegetables should be well covered), bring to the boil, then turn down the heat and simmer, covered, for at least 2 hours, until the beans are very soft.

Take out 2–3 large ladles of soup and mash well. Stir back into the soup to thicken it. Stir in the cavolo nero and leave to simmer for another 15 minutes.

Remove from the heat, let cool, then refrigerate overnight. The next day, slowly reheat the soup and stir in the remaining olive oil. Toast the bread and rub with garlic. Pile the bread in individual bowls and ladle the soup over the top. Serve with grated Parmesan.

An old-fashioned nourishing soup, full of healthy green things. If you do not have sorrel growing in your garden (or available in your supermarket), it can be omitted.

soupe du potager

1 fresh bay leaf

1 small cabbage, quartered

60 g butter

2 leeks, halved and sliced

1 onion, chopped

250 g new potatoes, chopped

a handful of chopped fresh flat leaf parsley

250 g fresh shelled peas

1 Little Gem lettuce, quartered and thinly sliced

a bunch of sorrel, sliced

salt and black pepper

unsalted butter and/or crème fraîche, to serve (optional)

serves 4–6

Put the bay leaf in a large saucepan of water and bring to the boil. Add the cabbage and blanch for 3 minutes. Drain the cabbage, pat dry and slice it thinly.

Heat the butter in a large saucepan. Add the cabbage, leeks, onion and 2 teaspoons salt and cook until softened, 5–10 minutes. Add the potatoes, parsley and 2 litres water. Season to taste and simmer gently for 40 minutes.

Stir in the peas, lettuce and sorrel and cook for 10 minutes more. Taste for seasoning. Ladle into bowls, add 1 tablespoon of butter and/or crème fraîche, if using, to each and serve.

This bright green soup is named after the beautiful river in Provence, north of Brignoles – the green minerals in the rocky bed make the water a wonderful colour. It can be served hot or cold – you will get maximum colour, flavour and goodness if you blend the herbs into the chilled soup.

soupe verdon

1 tablespoon sunflower oil

1 large onion, finely chopped

100 g potato, cut into dice

1 Golden Delicious apple, peeled and finely chopped

850 ml vegetable or chicken stock

a large bunch of watercress

a handful of fresh chervil

salt and black pepper

to serve

double cream or crème fraîche

avruga or other caviar (optional)

serves 4–6

Put the oil and onion in a saucepan, heat gently, then cook for 5 minutes until softened and translucent. Add the potato and apple, cover with a lid and continue cooking gently for a further 5 minutes. Add the stock and bring to the boil, lower the heat and simmer for 10 minutes. Season to taste.

Remove any thick or tough stalks from the watercress and remove the chervil stalks (which can taste over-grassy). Chop the watercress and chervil leaves and add to the soup. Simmer for 1 minute, then strain through a sieve into a clean pan. Put the solids from the sieve into a blender with a little of the liquid and process to a purée. Return to the pan and reheat gently.

Serve with a swirl of cream or crème fraîche and a spoonful of caviar, if using.

Here's a very good vegetable-only alternative to the usual tasty bouillabaisse that has fish and shellfish as a base. It has all the same flavours, including the best part – the chilli-spiked rouille sauce.

vegetable bouillabaisse

4 tablespoons olive oil

2 leeks, chopped

1 large onion, coarsely chopped

1 fennel bulb, chopped

3 garlic cloves, crushed

3 large ripe tomatoes, skinned, deseeded and chopped

5 new potatoes, chopped

2 litres vegetable stock

1 bay leaf

a sprig of fresh thyme

a strip of peel from 1 orange

1 teaspoon saffron strands

1 baguette, sliced, for croutons

100 g Gruyère cheese, grated

salt and black pepper

chopped fresh parsley, to serve

rouille

3 garlic cloves, finely chopped

1–2 red chillies, finely chopped

1 egg yolk, at room temperature

300 ml olive oil

serves 4–6

Heat the oil in a large saucepan. Add the leeks, onion and fennel and cook until just beginning to brown, about 10 minutes. Stir in the garlic, tomatoes, potatoes and 1 teaspoon salt and cook for 1 minute. Add the stock, the bay leaf, thyme, orange peel and saffron and stir. Bring to the boil, reduce the heat and simmer gently until the potatoes are tender, about 40 minutes. Season to taste, cover and let stand for at least 1 hour, or cool and refrigerate overnight.

Before you serve, make the croutons. Arrange the baguette slices in a single layer on a baking tray. Bake in a preheated oven at 180°C (350°F) Gas 4 until golden, about 5–8 minutes. Set aside.

To make the rouille, put the garlic, chillies and egg yolk in a small, deep bowl. Beat well. Add the oil bit by bit and beating vigorously, until the mixture is thick like mayonnaise.

To serve, warm the soup if necessary. Put 2–3 croutons in each soup plate, sprinkle with the grated cheese and ladle in the soup. Sprinkle with chopped parsley and serve with the rouille, to be stirred in according to taste.

Originating from the South of France, soupe au pistou is endlessly varied, but the constants are tomatoes, vegetables and the basil purée or 'pistou'. Stirred in at the end, it adds a heart-warming vibrancy to this hearty soup.

soupe au pistou

3 tablespoons olive oil

1 onion, chopped

1 small fennel bulb, chopped

2 courgettes, chopped

200 g new potatoes, chopped

2 tomatoes, skinned, deseeded and chopped

2 litres vegetable stock

a sprig of fresh thyme

400 g canned cannellini beans

400 g canned red kidney beans

150 g green beans, chopped

50 g spaghetti, broken up

150 g Gouda, grated, to serve

salt and black pepper

pistou

6 garlic cloves

a small bunch of fresh basil

6 tablespoons olive oil

serves 4–6

Heat the oil in a large saucepan. Add the onion, fennel and courgettes and cook over medium heat until browned, about 10 minutes. Add the potatoes, tomatoes, stock and thyme. Bring to the boil, then cover and simmer gently for 15 minutes.

Drain the cannellini and kidney beans, add to the pan and simmer, covered, for 15 minutes more. Taste and adjust the seasoning. Add the green beans and the spaghetti and cook until the pasta is tender, about 10 minutes more. Cover and let stand. Ideally, the soup should rest for at least a few hours before serving, or make it one day in advance and refrigerate.

Do not make the pistou until you are ready to serve. Put the garlic, basil and oil in a small food processor and blend until well chopped. You can also make it using a pestle and mortar, starting with the garlic and finishing with the oil, added gradually.

To serve, heat the soup and pass round the pistou and cheese, to be stirred in to taste. The soup can also be served at room temperature.

Artichokes can seem a little daunting, but in this recipe you don't have to worry about cutting out the fibrous, inedible bits – just cook them until they are soft enough to remove. The aromatic flavour of the tarragon combined with the Roquefort makes for a special soup.

globe artichoke, tarragon & Roquefort soup

juice of 1 lemon

8 large globe artichokes

1 tablespoon olive oil

25 g butter

1 large leek, sliced

1 garlic clove, chopped

2 tablespoons fresh tarragon leaves

500 ml vegetable stock

125 ml single cream

100 g Roquefort cheese, roughly crumbled

salt and black pepper

serves 4

Bring a large saucepan of water to the boil. Put the lemon juice and 1.5 litres water in a large bowl. Trim the leaves and stems from the artichokes. Cut each head in half and remove the hairy chokes. (Don't worry if you miss some of the gnarly bits, as they will come off more easily after cooking.) As you prepare each one, drop it in the bowl of water and lemon juice to prevent it from discolouring. When all the artichokes are prepared, add them to the pan of boiling water. Cook for 10–12 minutes and drain. Set aside. When cool enough to handle, trim the artichokes so that you are left with just the soft, fleshy bits.

Put the oil and butter in a large saucepan set over high heat. When the butter sizzles, add the leek and garlic, partially cover with a lid and cook for 5 minutes, until the leek sweats and softens. Add the tarragon and stir for 1 minute. Add the stock and bring to the boil. Add the artichokes and cook for 10 minutes. Transfer the mixture to a blender and whizz until smooth. Pour the mixture back into the saucepan set over low heat and gently reheat. Add the cream, season to taste and stir. Ladle the soup into warmed bowls, sprinkle with the Roquefort and serve.

The smoky flavours of the roasted aubergine and peppers make this tomato-based soup really enticing. Oregano is a perfect match to all these flavours with its woody aroma, and yes the soup really does need all that roasted garlic!

aubergine & red pepper soup

1 large aubergine

4 red peppers

2 sprigs of fresh thyme

1 garlic bulb, halved horizontally

2 tablespoons olive oil

1 red onion, cut into wedges

500 ml vegetable stock

300 g passata

a handful of fresh oregano leaves

salt and black pepper

to serve

fresh basil leaves

basil oil

serves 4–6

Preheat the oven to 190°C (375°F) Gas 5.

Put the whole aubergine and peppers in a large roasting tin. Sandwich the thyme between the garlic halves, drizzle with the oil, then wrap in foil and add to the tin. Roast in the preheated oven for 35 minutes.

Remove the garlic from the oven, checking it is tender first, and set aside to cool. Remove the peppers, transfer to a plastic bag, seal and leave to cool.

Add the onion to the roasting tin (still containing the aubergine) and roast for 20 minutes or until the aubergine feels tender when pierced with a knife.

Meanwhile, peel the skins off the cooled peppers and discard. Transfer the flesh to a blender and liquidize with a third of the stock until smooth. Transfer to a saucepan. Squeeze out the soft flesh from inside the garlic cloves and add to the blender. Spoon the flesh of the aubergine into the blender with the onion and another third of the stock. Blend until smooth, then add to the pepper purée in the saucepan. Add the passata, oregano and remaining stock and bring to the boil. Season to taste.

Divide the soup between 4–6 bowls, scatter with basil leaves and drizzle with basil oil.

A fresh, summery soup that can be adapted to other ingredients – it's also good with cauliflower and cannellini beans, or sweet potatoes and fresh borlottis. Feel free to use frozen broad beans. Like peas and corn, they are one of the few ingredients that are better frozen.

cream of broccoli soup with leeks & broad beans

2 tablespoons butter

2 tablespoons sunflower oil

2 large leeks, coarsely chopped

2 large heads broccoli, broken into florets

1 medium baking potato, chopped

600 ml vegetable or chicken stock

250 g shelled broad beans, fresh or frozen

salt and white pepper

basil oil, to serve

serves 4

Put the butter and oil in a large saucepan and heat until the butter melts. Add the leeks and fry gently until softened but not browned. Reserve a few spoonfuls of the cooked leeks for garnishing the soup.

Add the broccoli to the pan and stir-fry until bright green. Add the potato and stock and bring to the boil. Reduce the heat, season and simmer for 30 minutes, topping up with boiling water if necessary.

If using broad beans, cook in boiling salted water until just tender, then drain and transfer to a bowl of cold water. Pop the cooked beans out of their skins and discard – the bright green beans look and taste better. Reserve a few spoonfuls of broad beans for serving.

Strain the soup into a bowl and put the solids and remaining broad beans in a blender or food processor. Add 2 ladles of the strained liquid and purée until smooth. Add the remaining liquid and blend again. If the soup is too thick, thin it with water. Reheat the soup, pour into bowls, top with the reserved leeks and skinned broad beans, then serve with a trickle of basil oil over the top.

Note If you like, the potato may be omitted. Instead, peel the broccoli stalks, chop coarsely and add at the same time as the stock.

Squashes and allspice are native to the Americas and pine nuts have been gathered in the deserts of the south-west for at least a thousand years. This is a quintessentially American soup – the key is the light spicing and the roasting of the butternut squash to bring out the best of its sweet flavour.

allspice butternut squash soup

1 medium butternut squash, halved lengthways and deseeded

25 g butter

1 large leek, trimmed and chopped

1 fresh bay leaf

a few black peppercorns, crushed

4–5 allspice berries, crushed

600 ml vegetable stock

60 g pine nuts, lightly toasted in a dry frying pan

crusty bread, to serve

serves 4

Preheat the oven to 190°C (375°F) Gas 5.

Put the butternut squash halves flesh side down onto a baking sheet. Roast in the preheated oven for 45 mintues or until tender. Remove from the oven and, using a spoon, scoop the flesh out of the skins into a bowl. Discard the skins.

Put the butter into a large saucepan and melt over medium/low heat. Add the leek, bay leaf, peppercorns and allspice and fry gently until the leek begins to soften. Add the butternut squash, stock and 1 litre water. Bring to the boil, reduce the heat and simmer for about 10 minutes, or until the leeks are very soft.

Remove the bay leaf and transfer the soup to a blender. Add the pine nuts and process until smooth, working in batches if necessary. Return the soup to the saucepan and reheat. Serve hot with crusty bread.

This comforting soup also works well with pumpkin. The coconut milk makes the soup quite rich so it works well as a supper dish or followed by a light main course. Serve it with root vegetable crisps for added texture and flavour.

spiced butternut squash & coconut soup

25 g butter

1 white onion, roughly chopped

185 g carrots, peeled and roughly chopped

500 g butternut squash, peeled, deseeded and diced

½ teaspoon ground cumin

1 teaspoon Madras curry powder

400 ml vegetable stock

1 tablespoon muscovado sugar

170 ml canned coconut milk, plus extra to garnish

juice of ½ lime

salt and black pepper

a handful of chopped fresh coriander

serves 2–4

Melt the butter in a large saucepan over low heat. Add the onion, carrot and squash and gently fry for 5–8 minutes, stirring occasionally, until the vegetables begin to soften. Add the cumin and curry powder and stir over medium heat for 1 minute until the vegetables are well coated with the spices.

Stir in the stock, sugar and coconut milk and let simmer for about 20 minutes, or until the vegetables are cooked through and soft.

Put the soup in a blender and process until smooth. Season to taste then add the lime juice. Stir in the chopped coriander. Pour the soup into bowls, swirl some extra coconut milk over the top and serve.

Aromatherapy in a soup – this dish tastes marvellous. Purée it coarsely, so the brilliant carrot orange is just flecked with green. The bocconcini – little mouthfuls of mozzarella – peep out from just under the surface.

creamy carrot soup with herbs

3 leeks, thinly sliced

2 garlic cloves, crushed

1 tablespoon sunflower oil

600 g carrots, thinly sliced

1.25 litres vegetable stock

40 g bunch of chopped fresh sorrel

leaves from 4 sprigs each of fresh tarragon and basil

leaves from 6 sprigs each of fresh parsley and marjoram

to serve

100 ml crème fraîche

12 bocconcini, torn in half, or 2 regular mozzarella cheeses, torn into pieces

a handful of fresh chives

black pepper

serves 6

Put the leeks, garlic and oil in a small saucepan, cover with a lid and cook gently for 5 minutes. Add the carrots and cook gently for a further 5 minutes. Add the stock, bring to the boil and simmer for 5 minutes. Lower the heat, add the sorrel and simmer, uncovered, for a further 5 minutes.

Coarsely chop the tarragon, parsley, basil and marjoram. Stir into the soup. Strain the mixture through a sieve back into the saucepan and put the solids into a food processor or blender with a little of the liquid. Blend to a coarse purée, then return to the pan and reheat.

Remove from the heat and fold in the crème fraîche. Ladle into bowls and add a few bocconcini pieces to each one. Sprinkle with chives and pepper, then serve.

The delicate flavour of carrots is best blended with vegetable stock or water as chicken muddies their flavour of really good carrots. However, if you're doubtful of your carrots' flavour, go for a good chicken stock.

spiced carrot soup

50 g butter

1 onion, chopped

800 g carrots, chopped

2 teaspoons ground coriander

½ teaspoon ground ginger

¼ teaspoon chilli powder

1 litre vegetable stock or water

4 tablespoons double cream

2 tablespoons sunflower oil

5 cm fresh ginger, cut into matchsticks

salt and black pepper

serves 4

Melt the butter in a large saucepan and fry the onion for 5–8 minutes until softened. Add the carrots, ground coriander, ginger and chilli powder and stir into the butter to coat them and release the flavour of the spices. Season well, then pour in the stock. Simmer for 40 minutes.

Transfer the contents of the pan to a blender in batches (or use a handheld blender) and liquidize to a smooth purée. Stir in the cream. Add a little more water if it is too thick and season to taste.

Heat the oil in a frying pan over high heat and fry the ginger for 1 minute, or until crisp.

Divide the soup between 4 bowls and garnish with the ginger.

This soup can be served cold, in traditional vichyssoise fashion, or hot. If you don't have any ginger to hand, substitute white pepper, but add it at the end, so it keeps its zing.

carrot vichyssoise

a large pinch of saffron threads

2 large potatoes, about 350 g, cubed

500 ml chicken stock

2 tablespoons butter

2 tablespoons sunflower oil

1 large leek, chopped

2 garlic cloves, crushed

3 cm fresh ginger, peeled and finely grated

500 g carrots, grated

salt

to serve

4 tablespoons cream or crème fraîche

a handful of fresh chives

serves 4

Put the saffron in a small cup and cover with about 125 ml boiling water. Let steep for at least 20 minutes.

Meanwhile, put the potatoes in a saucepan, add the stock to cover and bring to the boil. Reserve the cooking liquid.

Next, melt the butter and oil in a frying pan, add the leeks and cook until softened. Transfer to a dish. Add a little more butter and oil to the pan, then the garlic, ginger and carrots. Simmer until done, then add the saffron and its soaking water. Transfer the leeks to the pan and simmer for about 5 minutes. Add the cooked potatoes and blend with a handheld blender. Stir in the potato cooking water. Season to taste. Let simmer for a further 5 minutes then add liquid to thin the soup to the desired consistency. Add more seasoning if necessary.

Ladle into bowls, add a swirl of cream or a spoonful of crème fraîche, then snip fresh chives over the top.

To serve cold, let the soup cool after blending, then refrigerate. It will thicken, so add some more cold water to get the required consistency.

This soup verges on being a fondue, thanks to the generous serving of Swiss Gruyère – perfect for wintry nights by the fire. You could keep it light and add no cheese at all, but that wouldn't be nearly as tasty or satisfying.

creamy cauliflower & Gruyère soup

2 tablespoons butter

1 onion, roughly chopped

1 celery stick, chopped

1 small cauliflower [about 1 kg], cut into small pieces

1.5 litres vegetable or chicken stock

250 ml double cream

200 g Gruyère cheese, grated, plus extra to serve

salt and black pepper

chopped fresh flat leaf parsley, to serve

serves 4

Heat the butter in a saucepan over high heat. Add the onion and celery and cook for 5 minutes, until the onion has softened but not browned.

Add the cauliflower pieces and stock and bring to the boil. Allow to boil for 25–30 minutes, until the cauliflower is really soft and breaking up in the stock.

Transfer the mixture to a blender and process the mixture in batches until smooth. Return the purée to the saucepan. Add the cream and cheese and cook over low heat, stirring constantly, until the cheese has all melted smoothly into the soup. Season to taste.

Serve sprinkled with chopped parsley and extra cheese.

This soup might require quite a few ingredients but the end result is worth it. The cauliflower absorbs the flavour of coconut, making it light and sweet. It's a dinner party pleaser that won't have you chained to the kitchen for too long at all.

cauliflower & coconut soup

600 ml coconut cream

2 stalks lemongrass, finely sliced

5 cm fresh galangal or ginger, peeled and finely sliced into rings

4 kaffir lime leaves, coarsely torn into quarters

1 small cauliflower, cut into florets

125 g small button mushrooms, cut into halves

3 tablespoons light soy sauce

1 teaspoon sugar

600 ml vegetable stock

4 small red or green chillies, slightly crushed

3 tablespoons lime juice

fresh coriander leaves, to serve

serves 4

Put the coconut cream, lemongrass, galangal, kaffir lime leaves, cauliflower, mushrooms, soy sauce, sugar and stock in a large saucepan and bring to the boil. Reduce the heat and simmer until the cauliflower is cooked, but still firm. Remove from the heat and add the chillies and lime juice. Stir once, pour into a serving bowl and top with coriander leaves.

Notes If you are unable to find coconut cream, use canned coconut milk instead. Don't shake the can – you will find it has probably separated into thick cream and thin milk. Carefully spoon off the thick part to use in recipes that specify coconut cream.

Galangal is widely available in markets selling South-east Asian produce. Fresh ginger is used as a common substitute in the West, though it has a totally different flavour.

Cauliflower has a gentle spiciness and creaminess which makes for wonderful soups. The Stilton can be replaced with Gorgonzola or Roquefort if you prefer. The Pear and Date Relish is a lovely touch and worth the extra effort if you have the time.

cauliflower & Stilton soup

1 large cauliflower (about 600 g), cut into florets

1 litre vegetable stock

25 g butter

1 onion, chopped

2 celery sticks, chopped

1 leek, chopped

4 sprigs of fresh thyme

4 dried bay leaves

150 g Stilton

75 ml crème fraîche

salt and black pepper

pear & date relish (optional)

25 g butter

3 tablespoons pine nuts

2 pears, peeled, cored and cut into 2-cm pieces

3 dates, finely chopped

75 ml cider vinegar

2 tablespoons soft brown sugar

serves 4

If you are making the relish, melt the butter in a saucepan over medium heat and add the pine nuts. Cook, stirring, for about 2 minutes. Add the pears, cover and cook for 2–3 minutes until softening. Add the dates, vinegar and sugar, season and cook for 10–15 minutes, uncovered, until the liquid has evaporated (add a splash of water if it dries too fast). Leave to cool a little before serving.

Put the cauliflower florets in a large saucepan with the stock. Bring to the boil and simmer until ready to use. Chop or break the florets into 5-cm pieces.

Melt the butter in another pan and cook the onion, celery and leek, covered, over low heat for 10–15 minutes until soft but not coloured.

Add the cauliflower, thyme leaves removed from their sprigs, bay leaves and seasoning. Strain the stock into the pan, discarding the bits and simmer for a further 20–25 minutes.

Transfer the contents of the pan, in batches, to a blender and liquidize until smooth, returning each batch back to the pan in which you cooked the stock. Place over low heat and add the Stilton and crème fraîche. Heat, stirring, until melted. Season to taste.

Divide the soup between 4 bowls and spoon the Pear and Date Relish over the top.

This soup is rich and elegant. It can be made dairy-free – use olive oil instead of butter and leave out the crème fraîche. Although the Parsley Gremolata is optional, it will lift the flavour of the soup and add some contrasting colour.

celeriac & orange soup

2 tablespoons butter
or olive oil

1 large onion, chopped

1 celeriac (about 750 g), peeled
and cut into dice

1 litre vegetable stock

½ teaspoon saffron strands,
lightly ground with a
pestle and mortar

1 tablespoon honey

grated zest and juice of
1 large orange

salt and black pepper

crème fraîche, to serve

parsley gremolata (optional)

1 garlic clove

1 teaspoon coarse
sea salt

a handful of fresh flat leaf
parsley

2 tablespoons olive oil

serves 4

Heat the butter or oil in a saucepan, add the onion and cook until softened. Add the celeriac, cover and cook for 10 minutes, stirring occasionally. Add the remaining ingredients. Bring to the boil, then simmer for 20 minutes until the vegetables are tender. Transfer the contents of the pan to a blender in batches (or use a handheld blender) and liquidize to a smooth purée.

If you are making the gremolata, put all the ingredients in a food processor or spice grinder and purée until smooth. Alternatively, use a pestle and mortar.

To serve, ladle the soup into bowls and spoon over the gremolata and crème fraîche.

This broth is bursting with the flavours of spring. To make it more substantial, you can add a scoop of risotto rice at the same time as the broad beans and a little more stock to compensate.

courgette, broad bean & lemon broth

2 tablespoons olive oil

1 unwaxed lemon

1 onion, chopped

3 tablespoons chopped fresh flat leaf parsley, plus extra to serve

500 g courgettes, sliced

300 g broad beans (podded weight)

800 ml chicken or vegetable stock

salt and black pepper

lemon olive oil, to serve (optional)

serves 4

Heat the oil in a large saucepan. Peel the zest from the lemon in one large piece so it's easy to find later and add that to the pan. Add the onion, parsley and courgettes, cover and cook over low heat, stirring occasionally, for 8 minutes or until softening.

Remove the lemon zest. Add the broad beans and stock, season well and return to the heat for a further 20 minutes.

Transfer a quarter of the soup to a blender, pulse until smooth, then stir back into the soup. Add some more salt and pepper if it needs it and lemon juice to taste.

Divide the soup between 4 bowls, drizzle with lemon oil, if using, and serve with extra parsley and a fresh grinding of black pepper.

The chilli content of this soup is rather conservative, but you can spice it up as much as you like. You can also purée it for a thicker, more chowder-like consistency.

courgette & corn soup

3 tablespoons olive oil

2 onions, halved, then sliced

3 courgettes, about 600 g, quartered lengthways, then sliced

2–3 potatoes, about 300 g, chopped

4 garlic cloves, sliced

2 corn-on-the-cob, kernels scraped with a knife

1 teaspoon ground cumin

1 red chilli, deseeded and sliced

1 litre chicken or vegetable stock

to serve

crème fraîche or cream

chopped fresh coriander

Tabasco sauce

serves 4

Heat the oil in a saucepan. Add the onions, courgettes, potatoes and some salt and cook over high heat until beginning to brown, about 5 minutes.

Add the garlic, corn, cumin and chilli and cook, stirring, for 1 minute more. Add the stock and 250 ml water. Bring to the boil, then lower the heat and simmer until the potatoes are tender, 15–20 minutes. Set aside for at least 30 minutes.

To serve, reheat the soup. Ladle into soup bowls and top each with a spoonful of crème fraîche, coriander and a dash of Tabasco. Serve immediately.

This deceptively creamy soup doesn't actually contain cream, making it lighter than it tastes. The fennel gives it a lovely aniseed flavour that complements the other vegetables perfectly.

fennel, leek & cauliflower soup

2 tablespoons olive oil

25 g butter

2 leeks, trimmed and sliced

1 large fennel bulb, trimmed and sliced (reserve the feathery leaves)

1 large garlic clove, crushed

1 small cauliflower

1 litre chicken or vegetable stock

1 bay leaf

2–3 sprigs of fresh tarragon or 1 teaspoon dried tarragon

2–3 tablespoons whole milk (optional)

a small pinch of mace

salt and black pepper

a few fresh fennel, dill or parsley leaves and some chives, to garnish

serves 6

Heat the oil for a minute or two in a large saucepan, then add the butter. When the foaming dies down, add the leeks, fennel and garlic, stir well, cover and cook over a low heat for about 8–10 minutes. Meanwhile, remove the florets from the cauliflower. Add them to the pan, stir and cook for another 3–4 minutes.

Pour the stock over the vegetables, add the bay leaf and tarragon and bring to the boil. Partially cover the pan and simmer for about 15 minutes or until the cauliflower and fennel are soft. Remove from the heat and allow to cool slightly. Remove the bay leaf and tarragon. Strain the soup, reserving the liquid.

Put the vegetables in a food processor and whizz until smooth, adding as much of the reserved liquid as you need to make a smooth, creamy consistency. Whizz the remaining liquid in the blender to pick up the last scraps of vegetable purée and add to the soup in the pan. Reheat gently, diluting the soup with a little more stock or milk if it seems too thick. Season to taste with salt, pepper and mace.

Chop the reserved fennel leaves or some dill or parsley and cut the chives into approximately 1½-cm lengths. Serve the soup in individual bowls, scatter with the herbs and serve.

The pearl barley in this Middle Eastern soup gives it a very satisfying bite. If you'd like it to have less of a kick, deseed the green chillies. The flavoured butter might seem a bit of a luxury but its blend of herbs and spices gives the soup added wow.

leek, barley & yoghurt soup

30 g butter

1 onion, finely chopped

3 leeks, thinly sliced

2 green chillies, chopped

1 tablespoon plain flour

100 g pearl barley

1.25 litres chicken stock

1 cinnamon stick

200 g Greek yoghurt

juice of ½ lemon

salt and black pepper

flavoured butter (optional)

75 g butter, softened

½ garlic clove, crushed

1 teaspoon sweet paprika

1 garlic clove, crushed

1 tablespoon chopped fresh mint

grated zest of 1 unwaxed lemon and juice of ½

serves 4

If you are making the flavoured butter, beat the butter until light and fluffy. Season; beat in the remaining ingredients and set aside.

For the soup, melt the butter in a heavy-based saucepan and fry the onion, leeks and chillies, covered, over low/medium heat for 10 minutes until softening. Stir occasionally so they don't catch or brown.

Add the flour and barley and stir around for 1 minute to toast slightly. Add the stock and cinnamon stick. Simmer for a further 30 minutes, until the barley is lovely and tender.

Remove the pan from the heat. In a separate bowl, beat the yoghurt and lemon juice with a ladleful of the liquid from the pan. Add this to the soup, beating it in, and return to a low heat. Cook, stirring, for just 2–3 minutes until warmed through, but don't let it boil.

Meanwhile, heat a frying pan and melt the flavoured butter until it starts to froth and continue to cook until golden.

Divide the soup between 4 bowls and spoon the butter over the top.

This velvety soup will suit all tastes and any occasion, from a quick supper for one to a dinner party. To ensure that the soup has a really smooth texture, make sure you blend then sieve it before serving.

leek & potato soup with watercress purée

75 g butter

2 medium onions, thinly sliced

500 g leeks (white part only), thinly sliced

175 g floury potatoes, chopped

1.3 litres chicken stock

300 ml milk

150 ml crème fraîche, plus extra to serve

salt and white pepper

watercress purée

125 g watercress, washed

5 tablespoons olive oil

serves 6

To make the purée, pick the leaves off the watercress stalks and put in a blender with the olive oil. Blend until smooth. Pour into a screwtop jar and set aside.

To make the soup, melt the butter in a large saucepan and add the onions and leeks. Stir well, add 3 tablespoons water, cover tightly and cook over gentle heat for 10 minutes until soft and golden.

Stir in the potatoes and chicken stock. Bring to the boil, reduce the heat, cover and simmer for 20 minutes until the potatoes are tender. Stir in the milk, then purée in a blender or with a handheld blender. Press the purée through a sieve, then return it to the pan.

Stir in the crème fraîche and season to taste. Cool and chill (if serving chilled, add extra seasoning) or serve hot with a swirl of watercress purée and a dollop of chilled crème fraîche.

Mushrooms and their earthiness blend really well with the sweet, mellow tang of Madeira wine. The toasted hazelnuts add a lovely thickness to the soup and another complementary flavour, but you can omit them if you prefer.

mushroom soup with Madeira

50 g butter

1 large onion, chopped

3 garlic cloves, crushed

25 g blanched hazelnuts

3 tablespoons chopped fresh flat leaf parsley

350 g chestnut or field mushrooms, sliced

25 g dried porcini mushrooms

1 litre vegetable or chicken stock

100 ml Madeira

serves 4–6

Melt the butter in a large saucepan and add the onion and garlic. Cover and cook over low heat for 10 minutes, or until soft. Stir occasionally so that they don't colour. Meanwhile, toast the hazelnuts in a dry frying pan and roughly chop, then set aside.

Add half the parsley and all the mushrooms to the saucepan and turn the heat up to medium. Cover and cook, stirring, for 15 minutes until they are softened.

Put the dried mushrooms in a heatproof bowl with 100 ml of the hot stock and set aside to soak for about 15 minutes to rehydrate.

Add the Madeira to the pan and cook until it evaporates. Add the remaining stock and the dried mushrooms with their soaking liquid, cover and cook for 10 minutes.

Transfer half the soup to a blender, along with half the hazelnuts and liquidize until smooth, then stir back into the pan and heat through.

Divide the soup between 4–6 bowls and scatter the remaining parsley and toasted hazelnuts over the top.

A few dried porcini will give a stronger flavour to a soup made with regular cultivated mushrooms. The roux gives a wonderful nutty aroma to the soup but can be omitted if you so desire.

cream of mushroom soup

25 g dried porcini mushrooms

4 tablespoons olive oil

6 large portobello mushrooms, wiped, trimmed and sliced

1 onion, halved and finely sliced

3 garlic cloves, crushed

a pinch of nutmeg

a large bunch of fresh flat leaf parsley, finely chopped

1.5 litres vegetable stock

salt and black pepper

roux

4 tablespoons butter

4 tablespoons plain flour

to serve

4–6 tablespoons coarsely chopped fresh flat leaf parsley

4–6 tablespoons crème fraîche

serves 4–6

Put the dried porcini in a bowl, add 250 ml boiling water and let soak for at least 15 minutes. Heat the oil in a frying pan, add the fresh mushrooms and sauté until coloured but still firm. Reserve a few slices for serving.

Add the onion to the frying pan and sauté until softened, then add the garlic, nutmeg and parsley. Rinse any grit out of the porcini and strain their soaking liquid several times through muslin or a tea strainer. Add the liquid and the porcini to the pan. Bring to the boil, then transfer to a food processor. Add 2 ladles of the boiling stock, then pulse until creamy but still chunky.

For the roux, heat the butter in a saucepan, stir in the flour and cook gently, stirring constantly, until the mixture is very dark brown (take care or it will burn). Add the remaining stock, 1 ladle at a time, stirring well after each addition. Add the mushroom mixture, bring to the boil, then simmer for 20 minutes. Season to taste, then serve topped with a few reserved mushrooms, parsley and a spoonful of crème fraîche.

Note If you use a blender to make the soup, the purée will be very smooth. If you use a food processor, it will be less smooth, and if you use the pulse button, you can make the mixture quite chunky, which suits mushrooms.

Similar to Gazpacho, this cold soup hailing from Malaga, Spain, makes a refreshing summer starter or light lunch. It is worth taking the time to refrigerate the soup for an hour or so to let the flavours combine and the garlic shine through.

ajo blanco

2 thick slices of stale white country-style bread, crusts removed

3 garlic cloves, peeled

150 g blanched almonds, very finely ground

150 ml extra virgin olive oil

2 tablespoons sherry vinegar (or to taste)

a small bunch of white grapes, halved

salt and black pepper

serves 2–4

Soak the bread in a little water for 5 minutes or so to soften it. Squeeze out the excess water and transfer the bread to a food processor. Add the garlic, ground almonds and 800 ml water and whizz until smooth. Season to taste. If possible, refrigerate the soup for an hour or so to allow the lovely garlicky flavour to develop.

Stir in 100 ml of the olive oil and the sherry vinegar, adjust the seasoning if necessary and spoon into four chilled bowls. Drizzle the soup with the remaining olive oil and garnish with white grapes. This is lovely served with toasted country-style bread, drizzled with some more extra virgin olive oil.

There aren't many ingredients in this soup, so you need to get the caramelization of the onions spot on – cook them slowly and then once soft, turn up the heat and cook until a sticky golden brown. The stock needs to be richly flavoured or the soup will be insipid.

French onion soup

50 g butter

1 kg onions, sliced

2 garlic cloves, crushed

1 tablespoon granulated sugar

2 tablespoons Cognac or brandy

300 ml dry cider

1.25 litres beef stock

1 bouquet garni (1 sprig each of fresh parsley, thyme and bay)

salt and black pepper

garlic toasts

4 tablespoons extra virgin olive oil

1 garlic clove, crushed

1 small baguette or ½ large baguette, sliced

200 g Gruyère cheese, grated

serves 4

Preheat the oven to 180°C (350°F) Gas 4.

To make the garlic toasts, mix the oil and garlic together and season well. Arrange the baguette slices on a baking tray and brush with the garlic oil. Bake in the preheated oven for 25 minutes until crisp.

Melt the butter in a large saucepan or casserole over medium heat. Add the onions and garlic and stir until starting to soften. Turn the heat to low, cover and cook gently for 25–30 minutes until really softened.

Take the lid off and add the sugar. Cook for a further 20 minutes, stirring until golden brown and extremely soft. Pour in the Cognac and cider and leave to bubble up for 1 minute. Add the stock and bouquet garni and stir to blend. Simmer for 45 minutes, then season to taste. Remove the bouquet garni.

Preheat the grill.

Divide the soup between 4 ovenproof bowls and place them on a baking tray. Float 2–3 garlic toasts on top of each bowl and scatter the Gruyère over the toasts. Grill until the Gruyère is bubbling and golden. Remove the baking tray and lift off the hot bowls using an oven glove, warning everyone that they are hot.

This is loosely based on the Venetian dish *risi e bisi*, which uses new season peas. It's a cross between a soup and a risotto and should be soupy in consistency. Just omit the pancetta if you would like to serve it to vegetarians – it's tasty enough without it.

minty pea risotto soup

30 g butter

1 onion, finely chopped

150 g pancetta, cubed

400 g frozen peas, defrosted, or fresh if available

2 tablespoons extra virgin olive oil, plus extra for drizzling

150 g risotto rice

1.5 litres chicken or vegetable stock, plus extra if necessary

2 tablespoons fresh mint, shredded

salt and black pepper

freshly grated Parmesan cheese, to serve

serves 4–6

Melt the butter in a medium saucepan, then add the onion and pancetta. Cook over low/medium heat, with the lid on, for 8 minutes, or until the onion is softened and translucent. Stir occasionally.

Meanwhile, put half the peas in a food processor with the olive oil and blend until puréed.

Add the rice to the softening onion and stir until well coated in butter. Pour in the stock and add the puréed peas. Simmer, uncovered, for 15 minutes.

Add the remaining peas, season well and cook for a further 8–10 minutes, or until the rice is tender. Stir in the mint and add a little more stock if you think it needs to be soupier.

Transfer to bowls, drizzle with olive oil and scatter with freshly ground black pepper. Serve with grated Parmesan cheese.

The best way to tackle a pumpkin is to place it on a chopping board and, keeping your hands well clear, hack into it with a large, sharp knife. First split it in half, then once you have a flat side, slice it into large chunks. Peel with an upright peeler and chop the flesh.

pumpkin & coconut soup

1 kg pumpkin or butternut squash, peeled, deseeded and cut into 3-cm dice

1 onion, cut into wedges

½ teaspoon dried chilli flakes

1 teaspoon ground coriander

1 teaspoon ground ginger

4 tablespoons extra virgin olive oil

3 whole garlic cloves, peeled

800 ml chicken stock

100 ml coconut milk

2 tablespoons fish sauce

juice of 1 lime

black pepper

to serve

double cream

chopped red chillies (optional)

serves 4–6

Preheat the oven to 200°C (400°F) Gas 6.

Put the pumpkin, onion, chilli flakes, coriander, ginger and olive oil in a large roasting tin and toss well. Cover with aluminium foil and roast in the preheated oven for 40 minutes, stirring halfway through, until almost soft.

Remove the foil and discard, add the garlic cloves and return to the oven for a further 20 minutes or until the garlic is tender.

Transfer the contents of the roasting tin to a blender and liquidize with half the stock until smooth. Return to the pan and add the remaining stock and the coconut milk. Bring to the boil and simmer for about 10 minutes to allow the flavours to mingle. Stir in the fish sauce and lime juice and taste for seasoning – if it needs more salt, add a dash more fish sauce.

Divide the soup between 4–6 bowls, drizzle with cream and finish with a fresh grinding of black pepper or some chopped red chillies. Serve with some country-style bread on the side.

If you are making this soup for children, omit the chillies and use 500 ml milk mixed with 500 ml stock. The inclusion of paprika and garlic will ensure that it still has a lot of flavour.

spicy red pepper & tomato soup

6 medium red peppers, roughly chopped

375 g carrots, roughly chopped

1–2 red chillies, deseeded and halved

750 g ripe plum tomatoes

3 large garlic cloves, peeled

6 tablespoons olive oil

2 teaspoons smoked sweet paprika

1.25 litres vegetable or beef stock

salt and black pepper

crisply fried bacon slices, to serve

serves 8

Preheat the oven to 200°C (400°F) Gas 6.

Put the peppers, carrots, chillies, tomatoes and garlic in a large roasting tin, then toss them in the oil. Season well and roast in the preheated oven for about 30 minutes until all the vegetables are soft and slightly charred at the edges.

Transfer half the vegetables to a blender, add the paprika and half the stock and blend until smooth. Pour into a saucepan and repeat with the remaining vegetables and stock, adding extra stock if it seems too thick. Reheat until almost boiling, add salt and pepper to taste, then serve with the bacon on top.

If you love truffle oil, this is a great excuse to use some of that treasured bottle. If you don't, it is perfectly fine without it. The egg is also optional but does add a lovely splash of colour.

rocket soup with poached egg & truffle oil

25 g butter

2 leeks, chopped

250 g potatoes, peeled and chopped

1 litre chicken stock

200 g wild rocket

1 teaspoon white wine vinegar

4 eggs

100 ml double cream

salt and black pepper

1–2 tablespoons truffle oil, to serve

serves 4

Melt the butter in a large, heavy-based saucepan and add the leeks. Cover and cook over low heat for 8 minutes until softening and glistening. Add the potatoes and cook, covered, for a further 5 minutes. Pour in the stock and simmer for 15 minutes or until the potatoes are really tender. Remove from the heat and add the rocket, then let it wilt for 10 minutes.

Meanwhile, bring a deep frying pan of water to the boil, add the vinegar, then turn down to a gentle simmer. Crack the eggs in each corner and turn off the heat. Leave to sit for 3 minutes.

Transfer the soup to a blender and liquidize until smooth. Return to the pan, stir in the cream and season to taste.

Divide the soup between 4 bowls, top each with a poached egg and serve with a fresh grinding of black pepper and a drizzle of truffle oil.

Spinach, eggs and butter always work well together and this broth is no exception. It can be ready in under 10 minutes, making it the perfect dish to serve when time is against you.

spinach broth with egg

700 g fresh spinach

50 g butter

4 eggs

5 tablespoons freshly grated Parmesan cheese

¼ teaspoon freshly grated nutmeg

1.75 litres chicken stock

salt and black pepper

serves 6

Remove all the stalks from the spinach, then wash the leaves thoroughly – do not shake dry. Cook the leaves in a large saucepan. When the leaves have wilted, drain well, then chop finely.

Heat the butter in a medium saucepan, then add the spinach, tossing well to coat with the butter. Remove from the heat and let cool for 5 minutes.

Put the eggs, Parmesan, nutmeg, salt and pepper in a bowl and beat well. Mix into the spinach. Put the stock in a large saucepan and bring almost to the boil. When almost boiling, whisk in the spinach and egg mixture as quickly as you can to avoid curdling. Reheat gently without boiling for a couple of minutes and serve immediately.

Spring greens work very nicely with the simple Asian flavours here. This is a substantial soup – really more of a light stew. If you fancy eating it in true Asian style, serve it for breakfast.

garlic & chilli rice soup with spring greens

1 tablespoon vegetable oil

2 teaspoons sesame oil

2 garlic cloves, chopped

4 spring onions, finely chopped

2 teaspoons grated fresh ginger

1 small red chilli, deseeded and thinly sliced

100 g long-grain white rice

1.5 litres vegetable stock

1 tablespoon soy sauce or fish sauce

a bunch of spring greens, roughly shredded

a small bunch of chopped fresh coriander

white pepper

serves 2

Put the oils in a saucepan set over high heat. Add the garlic and spring onions and cook until the garlic is turning golden and just starting to burn. This will give the soup a lovely, nutty garlic flavour. Add the ginger, chilli and rice and stir-fry in the garlic-infused oil for 1 minute. Add the stock and soy sauce and bring to the boil

Cover with a lid and cook over low heat for 30 minutes, until the rice is soft and the soup has thickened. Add the spring greens and cook for 5 minutes, until they turn emerald green and are tender. Ladle the soup into warmed serving bowls, sprinkle the coriander over the top and season to taste with pepper.

This is a variation on a traditional Japanese summer soup with fresh corn playing centre stage. It's incredibly quick to make and quite filling too, thanks to the addition of egg yolks.

Japanese fresh corn soup

4 corn-on-the-cob or about 500 g fresh corn kernels

1 litre chicken stock

4 egg yolks

to serve

4 spring onions, sliced diagonally

2 tablespoons dark soy sauce

black pepper

serves 4

Bring a large saucepan of water to the boil, add the corn and simmer for about 2 minutes. Drain. Hold the corn upright on a chopping board, blunt end down. Run a sharp knife down the cobs, shaving off the kernels. Reserve a few sliced-off sections of kernels for serving, blanching them in boiling water for 2 minutes.

Put the remaining kernels in a blender with 250 ml of the stock. Purée until smooth, then press through a strainer into a saucepan. Return the corn to the blender, add another ladle of stock, purée, then strain as before, pushing through as much corn juice as possible. Repeat until all the stock has been used. Reheat the mixture, then remove from the heat.

Put 1 egg yolk into each of 4 small soup bowls, ladle the soup on top and beat with chopsticks (the hot soup cooks the egg). Alternatively, whisk all 4 egg yolks in a mixing bowl, beat into the soup, then ladle into bowls. Serve, topped with spring onions, the reserved kernel sections, soy sauce and pepper to taste.

Sweetcorn and cream are a match made in heaven. Do take the time to make the Red Pepper Tapenade if you can – it adds wonderful depth of flavour to this soup and can be put to many other uses too.

summer sweetcorn soup

8 corn-on-the-cobs

1 onion, chopped

1 celery stick, chopped

2 garlic cloves, chopped

40 g butter

1.5 litres vegetable stock

125 ml single cream

salt and black pepper

a small bunch of fresh chives, snipped, to serve

red pepper tapenade (optional)

1 large red pepper

1 garlic clove, chopped

50 g pine nuts, lightly toasted

2 tablespoons olive oil

50 g finely grated Parmesan cheese

serves 4

If making the tapenade, preheat the oven to 220°C (425°F) Gas 7. Put a baking tray in the oven for a few minutes to heat. Put the red pepper on the tray and cook it in the preheated oven for about 15 minutes, turning often until the skin is starting to blacken. Transfer it to a plastic bag and let cool. When the pepper is cool enough to handle, peel off the skin and discard, roughly chop the flesh and put it in a food processor. Add the garlic, pine nuts and oil and process until smooth. Spoon into a bowl, add the Parmesan and stir to combine.

Carefully shuck the corn kernels from the cobs and put them in a large saucepan. Add the onion, celery, garlic and butter and season well with salt and pepper. Set over medium heat and partially cover with a lid. Cook for 10 minutes, shaking the pan often. Add the stock, bring to the boil and let boil for 15 minutes. Remove from the heat and let cool for about 20 minutes.

Transfer the mixture to a blender and whizz until smooth. You may need to do this in batches. Force it through a fine sieve and return it to the saucepan. Add the cream and gently reheat, stirring constantly.

Ladle the soup into bowls, top with a dollop of Red Pepper Tapenade (if using), sprinkle with chives and serve.

Sweet potatoes make an excellent ingredient for soups. When blended they take on a velvety, creamy texture. Here, their sweetness is cut through with some full-on and spicy Asian flavours in the form of a Thai-style pesto, which really brings this soup to life.

sweet potato & coconut soup

1 tablespoon olive oil

500 g sweet potato, chopped

1 red onion, chopped

1 tablespoon red curry paste

500 ml vegetable stock

500 ml coconut milk

thai pesto

100 g unsalted peanuts, toasted

2 garlic cloves, chopped

2 teaspoons grated fresh ginger

2 large green chillies, deseeded and chopped

a small bunch of fresh coriander

a large handful of fresh mint

a large handful of fresh basil

2 tablespoons light soy sauce

2 tablespoons lime juice

1 tablespoon light brown sugar

serves 4

Put the oil in a heavy-based saucepan set over medium heat. Add the sweet potato and onion, partially cover with a lid and cook for 15 minutes, stirring often, until they are soft and just starting to turn golden. Increase the heat to high, add the curry paste and stir-fry with the sweet potato for 3–4 minutes so that the paste cooks and becomes fragrant. Add the stock and coconut milk and bring to the boil. Transfer the mixture to a food processor or blender and whizz until smooth. Return the soup to the saucepan.

To make the pesto, put all of the ingredients in a blender and whizz until you have a chunky green paste and the ingredients are all evenly chopped. Gently reheat the soup, then ladle into bowls. Top with a generous spoonful of Thai Pesto to serve.

This soup may take a while to make but it is worth waiting for – the tomatoes need all that time in the oven to grow beautifully sweet. The addition of rarebit toasts make this an ideal winter warmer.

roasted tomato soup with rarebit toasts

1 kg Italian tomatoes, such as Roma, halved

2 small red onions, quartered

6 sprigs of fresh lemon thyme

1 teaspoon white sugar

1 teaspoon sea salt

2 garlic cloves, sliced

2 tablespoons olive oil

500 ml vegetable stock

salt and black pepper

rarebit toasts

100 g mature Cheddar cheese, grated

3 tablespoons wheat beer

1 tablespoon Worcestershire sauce

4 slices of wholemeal bread or baguette

serves 4

Preheat the oven to 160°C (325°F) Gas 3.

Put the tomatoes, onion, lemon thyme, sugar, salt, garlic and oil in a large bowl. Use your hands to toss the ingredients to combine and evenly coat them in the oil. Tip the mixture out onto a baking tray and roast in the preheated oven for 1½ hours. Discard the lemon thyme sprigs then put the tomatoes, onions and any tasty juices in a blender and process until smooth, adding a little stock if the mixture is too thick to process. Transfer to a large saucepan, add the stock and cook over gentle heat for 10 minutes. Season to taste and keep warm.

Preheat the grill to high. Put the Cheddar, beer and Worcestershire sauce in a small saucepan set over low heat. Stir until the cheese has melted and the mixture is smooth. Toast the bread under the preheated grill on one side only. Spread about 2 tablespoons of the cheese mixture on each untoasted side of bread and grill until it is bubbling and golden. Cut into fingers and serve with the soup.

This soup is ready in minutes and is packed with flavour thanks to the pesto, lemon and fresh herbs. It's very pleasing on the eye too. Why not serve it with some ciabatta to complete the Italian theme?

tomato & pesto soup

1 kg very ripe tomatoes

500 ml chicken stock

salt and black pepper

to serve

shredded zest and juice of 1 unwaxed lemon

4 tablespoons basil pesto

scissor-snipped fresh chives or torn basil

serves 4

To skin the tomatoes, cut a cross in the base of each and dunk into a saucepan of boiling water. Remove after 10 seconds and put into a strainer set over a large saucepan. Slip off and discard the skins and cut the tomatoes in half around their 'equators'. Using a teaspoon, deseed into the strainer, then press the pulp and juice through the strainer and add to the blender. Discard the seeds. Chop the tomato halves and add to the blender.

Purée the tomatoes, adding a little of the stock to help the process – you may have to work in batches. Add the remaining stock, season to taste and transfer to the saucepan. Heat well without boiling. Serve in bowls topped with a spoonful of lemon juice, pesto, chives or basil, lemon zest and pepper.

The trick with tomato soup is to get a bit of acidity fighting back against the natural sweetness of the tomato. So you need sweet tomatoes, but to be sure you can add some sugar to taste to compensate. The vinegar will then cut through this sweetness.

tomato, chilli & rosemary soup

2 red onions, chopped

3 garlic cloves, crushed

4 tablespoons extra virgin olive oil

2 kg plum tomatoes, roughly chopped

1–2 tablespoons light brown sugar

2 tablespoons red wine vinegar

750 ml vegetable stock

salt and black pepper

chilli and rosemary oil (optional)

2 sprigs of fresh rosemary

150 ml extra virgin olive oil

3 large red chillies, deseeded and finely chopped

serves 4

If making the oil, put the rosemary and oil in a small saucepan and heat gently for 5 minutes. Remove from the heat, add the chillies and leave to cool. Season to taste. Transfer to a clean, lidded jar, seal and chill for up to 2 days.

Put the onions, garlic and oil in a large saucepan, cover and cook over low heat for 10 minutes, stirring occasionally until soft. Do not let them brown.

Add the tomatoes, sugar, vinegar and stock and season well. Bring to the boil, then turn down the heat and simmer for 30 minutes, stirring occasionally.

Transfer to a blender in batches and liquidize until really smooth.

Serve in bowls drizzled with Chilli and Rosemary Oil.

Despite taking no time at all to prepare, there is something about watercress that seems quintessentially English and refined. Its mustardy bite sits nicely with the intensely flavoured Gorgonzola. Serve this as a starter when you want to make a good impression.

watercress & pea soup

a small bunch of watercress, about 300 g

50 g butter

1 onion, chopped

1 celery stick, chopped

100 g wild rocket leaves

½ teaspoon cracked black pepper

300 g peas (frozen or freshly shelled)

1.5 litres vegetable stock

100 g Gorgonzola cheese (optional)

serves 4

Pick over the watercress to remove any discoloured leaves. Cut off and discard about 5 cm from the bottom of the stems. Roughly chop the leaves and remaining stems and set aside.

Put the butter in a large saucepan set over high heat and melt until sizzling. Add the onion and celery and cook for 2–3 minutes, until softened. Add the watercress, rocket and pepper and stir-fry for a couple of minutes until the greens wilt and start to pop in the hot pan. Add the peas and stock and bring to the boil. Reduce the heat and cook at a rapid simmer for 10 minutes, until all the vegetables are very soft. Transfer to a blender and whizz until smooth. Pass the mixture through a sieve back into the saucepan and gently reheat.

Cut the Gorgonzola into 4 pieces (if using) and put 1 in the bottom of each of 4 warmed serving bowls. Ladle the hot soup over the top and serve immediately.

pulses

This soup is quick and easy to throw together, yet it tastes so rich and herby that you would be forgiven for thinking it was the result of a real labour of love. It's high in protein too.

full of beans soup

750 g ripe tomatoes, halved

2 tablespoons chopped fresh basil leaves

2–3 garlic cloves, crushed

400 g canned mixed beans, drained and rinsed

100 g canned red kidney beans, drained and rinsed

1 vegetable stock cube

salt and black pepper

to serve

crème fraîche (optional)

freshly grated Parmesan cheese

1 tablespoon chopped fresh basil leaves

serves 4

Preheat the grill.

Put the tomatoes in a large roasting tin, cut sides up. Sprinkle with the basil and garlic, then season well. Grill for 5–10 minutes, until the tomatoes have softened.

Remove the tomatoes from the grill and let cool slightly. When cool enough to handle, peel the tomatoes, discarding the skins. Put the tomatoes in a food processor or blender and process until smooth. Add the mixed beans and kidney beans and process for a further 30 seconds, until the beans are broken down slightly but the soup still has a chunky texture.

Transfer the mixture to a saucepan. Dissolve the stock cube in 150 ml boiling water. Add the stock to the soup and heat gently over medium heat until piping hot, stirring occasionally.

Ladle the soup into bowls. Serve topped with 1 dessertspoon of crème fraîche, if using, a sprinkling of freshly grated Parmesan and some chopped basil.

Variation To make this soup even quicker, substitute the fresh tomatoes for 1 kg canned tomatoes. Don't forget to add plenty of fresh herbs. Use coriander instead of basil, if you prefer.

This satisfying minestrone is made more substantial by serving it with thick, garlicky toasted ciabatta. Using canned rather than dried beans makes for a speedy cooking time.

Swiss chard & white bean broth

2 tablespoons butter

1 onion, chopped

1 small bunch Swiss chard (about 350 g), finely chopped

1 litre vegetable stock

400 g canned cannellini beans, drained but not rinsed and roughly mashed

4 thick slices ciabatta

2 garlic cloves, peeled but left whole

olive oil, for drizzling

finely grated Parmesan cheese

serves 4

Heat the butter in a saucepan over medium heat. Add the onion and cook for 4–5 minutes to soften. Add the Swiss chard and cook for 5 minutes, stirring often until very soft. Add the stock and beans and gently bring to the boil. Season to taste.

Toast the ciabatta until golden on both sides. Rub the cut side of the bread with the garlic then place each into a serving bowl. Drizzle each piece of bread with the olive oil and ladle over the soup. Sprinkle the Parmesan on top.

Variation It's easy to turn this into a satisfying pasta meal. Simply omit the stock and add 400 g cooked pasta shapes to the pan when you add the beans, season well and stir through some finely grated Parmesan for extra flavour.

This simple soup is found in various guises all over central and northern Italy. The garlic, rosemary and chilli oil lends it a touch of sophistication and will fill your kitchen with a delicious aroma. It can be served as a main ladled over toasted country-style bread.

Tuscan bean soup

250 g dried white or brown beans (such as haricot, borlotti or cannellini)

a pinch of bicarbonate of soda

chicken or vegetable stock

a handful of fresh sage leaves, plus 2 tablespoons chopped fresh sage

4 garlic cloves, 2 cloves finely chopped, 2 cloves finely sliced

300 ml olive oil

2 tablespoons chopped fresh rosemary

a large pinch of dried chilli flakes

salt and black pepper

coarsely chopped fresh flat leaf parsley, to serve

serves 6

Put the beans in a bowl, cover with cold water, add a pinch of bicarbonate of soda, soak overnight, then drain just before you're ready to use them.

Preheat the oven to 160°C (325°F) Gas 3.

Put the drained beans in a flameproof casserole. Cover with stock to a depth of 5 cm above the beans, and add the sage. Bring to the boil, cover tightly with a lid and transfer to the preheated oven for about 1 hour or until tender. (The time depends on the freshness of the beans – test after 40 minutes.) Keep them in their cooking liquid.

Put half the beans, the cooked sage (minus any stalks), and all the liquid into a blender and whizz until smooth. Pour back into the remaining beans in the casserole. Add a little extra water or stock if the soup is looking too thick.

Heat half the oil in a frying pan and add the chopped garlic. Fry gently until soft and golden, then add the sage and cook for 30 seconds. Stir this into the soup and reheat until boiling. Simmer gently for 10 minutes. Season to taste and pour into 6 bowls.

Heat the remaining oil in a frying pan, add the sliced garlic and fry carefully until golden. Stir in the rosemary and chilli flakes. Spoon the garlic and oil over the soup, sprinkle with parsley and serve.

This wonderful, comforting soup hails from Campania, Italy, and combines two of the great storecupboard stand-bys – beans and pasta. It's low on fresh ingredients meaning it's cheap to make.

pasta & bean soup

185 g dried cannellini or haricot beans

a pinch of bicarbonate of soda

4 tablespoons olive oil, plus extra to serve

2 garlic cloves, crushed

1.75 litres chicken stock

100 g short pasta shapes, such as maccheroni or tubetti

4 tomatoes, skinned, deseeded and coarsely chopped

4 tablespoons chopped fresh flat leaf parsley

salt and black pepper

serves 6

Put the beans in a bowl, cover with cold water, add a pinch of bicarbonate of soda, soak overnight, then drain just before you're ready to use them.

The next day, put the drained beans in a large saucepan. Add the oil, garlic and stock. Bring to the boil, reduce the heat and simmer, part-covered with a lid, for 1–2 hours or until the beans are tender.

Working in batches if necessary, combine the beans with the cooking liquid using a blender. Return the bean purée to the pan, adding extra water or stock as necessary. Add the pasta and simmer gently for 15 minutes until tender. Add a little extra water or stock if the soup is looking too thick. Stir in the tomatoes and parsley and season well. Serve with an extra trickle of olive oil.

This soup gets its name from the red, green and white beans that are used to make it; the colours of the Italian flag. It's perfect on a cold winter's day and uses canned beans so it's ready in no time. Vegetable and chicken stock both work well in this recipe.

flag bean soup

1 tablespoon olive oil, plus extra to taste

3 large garlic cloves, 2 sliced, 1 crushed

1 large onion, finely chopped

250 g Puy lentils

1 litre chicken or vegetable stock, plus extra to taste

100 g canned butter beans

200 g canned green flageolet beans

200 g canned red kidney beans

200 g canned haricot or cannellini beans

salt and black pepper

to serve

fresh parsley or basil leaves

basil or olive oil

grated lemon zest (optional)

serves 4

Heat the oil in a frying pan, add the sliced garlic and fry gently on both sides until crisp and golden. Remove and drain on kitchen paper.

Add the onion and crushed garlic to the frying pan, adding extra oil if necessary, and cook gently until softened and transparent. Add the lentils and half the stock. Cook until the lentils are just tender.

Meanwhile, rinse and drain all the beans. Put them in a sieve and dunk the sieve in a large saucepan of boiling water. The beans are cooked – you are just reheating them.

Add the hot beans to the lentils, along with the remaining stock. Season to taste. If the soup is too thick, add extra boiling stock or water. Ladle into bowls, top with the reserved fried garlic and the herbs, add a few drops of basil oil and the lemon zest, if using, then serve with crusty bread.

This hearty soup is a meal in itself. Chunks of chorizo sit alongside chickpeas and spinach in a slightly smoky, fragrant broth. The special flavour comes from two typically Spanish spices, oak-smoked paprika and saffron.

Andalusian chickpea soup

2 tablespoons olive oil

1 onion, chopped

3 celery sticks, chopped, leaves reserved

1 carrot, chopped

2 garlic cloves, chopped

250 g chorizo cut into 1-cm slices

400 g canned chickpeas, drained and rinsed

1.75 litres chicken stock

¼ teaspoon Spanish oak-smoked paprika

125 g spinach leaves

¼ teaspoon saffron threads, bruised with a pestle and mortar

Manchego or Parmesan cheese, shaved, to serve (optional)

serves 4 as a main course

Heat the oil in a large saucepan and add the onion, celery and carrot. Gently fry the vegetables until they begin to soften. Add the garlic, chorizo, chickpeas, stock and paprika. Bring to the boil, reduce the heat and simmer for about 10 minutes. Add the spinach and celery leaves and simmer for a further 15 minutes.

Add the saffron to the saucepan and simmer for another 5 minutes. Serve in large, wide bowls as a main course. Add shavings of cheese, if using.

Picking wild mushrooms is a late-summer-to-autumn passion for all Italians. Wild mushrooms have a strong, earthy taste – almost meaty. The combination of creamy chickpeas and earthy mushrooms is unusual and absolutely captivating.

cream of chickpea soup with wild mushrooms

50 g butter

50 g pancetta

150 g fresh wild mushrooms or dark portobello mushrooms, plus 25 g dried porcini mushrooms, soaked in warm water for 20 minutes to soften

2 shallots, finely chopped

2 garlic cloves, coarsely chopped

juice of 1 lemon

400 g canned chickpeas, drained and rinsed

1.5 litres chicken or vegetable stock

150 ml double cream

3 tablespoons chopped fresh flat leaf parsley

salt and black pepper

serves 6

Put the butter in a large saucepan, melt gently, then add the pancetta and fry slowly until golden.

Put the mushrooms, shallots and garlic in a food processor and pulse until finely chopped. Add the mushroom mixture to the pancetta and cook, stirring over medium/high heat, for about 15 minutes, until all the juices have evaporated and the mixture becomes a thick paste. Stir in the lemon juice and chickpeas. Whisk in the stock and bring to the boil. Cover and simmer for 25 minutes.

Transfer the soup, in batches if necessary, to a blender and process until smooth. Return the soup to the pan and stir in the cream. Season to taste, then stir in the parsley and reheat without boiling, to stop the soup from curdling.

This storecupboard-based soup couldn't be easier. It's made from a minimal number of ingredients, but has a complex flavour. The addition of mint makes it refreshing, too.

chickpea, lemon & mint soup

1.2 kg canned chickpeas

2 garlic cloves, crushed

grated zest and juice of 2 unwaxed lemons

3 tablespoons chopped fresh mint

2 tablespoons extra virgin olive oil

salt and black pepper

serves 4

Drain the liquid from the chickpeas into a jug, and make it up to 750 ml with water. Tip two-thirds of the drained chickpeas into a food processor. Add the garlic, lemon zest and juice, mint, oil and enough of the chickpea liquid to blend to a purée. Pour into a saucepan and stir in the remaining whole chickpeas and liquid. Season to taste and heat through for about 5 minutes until gently bubbling. Ladle into bowls and serve immediately.

Often thought of as cold weather fare, this minestrone has summer written all over it and is packed with fresh flavours. The peppery bite of the rocket lightens the soup, making it much more than just another minestrone.

chickpea, tomato & green bean minestrone

2 tablespoons olive oil

1 onion, chopped

2 garlic cloves, chopped

400g canned chickpeas, drained and rinsed

100 g green beans, sliced on the angle

6 ripe tomatoes, halved

a handful of chopped fresh flat leaf parsley

1.5 litres vegetable stock

100 g wholemeal spaghetti, broken into 3–4-cm pieces

50 g wild rocket leaves

salt and black pepper

50 g pecorino or Parmesan cheese, finely grated, to serve

serves 4

Put the oil in a large saucepan set over medium heat. Add the onion, partially cover with a lid and cook for 4–5 minutes, stirring often, until softened. Add the garlic and cook for 1 minute. Add the chickpeas, beans, tomatoes, parsley, stock and spaghetti and bring to the boil.

Reduce the heat and let simmer for 40 minutes, stirring often, until the pasta is cooked and the soup is thick. Season to taste.

Just before serving, add the rocket and gently stir until the rocket wilts. Ladle into serving bowls and serve sprinkled with a generous amount of grated pecorino over the top.

Variation Try making this delicious soup with different vegetables. Courgettes and carrots are a nice addition but remember that both take a little longer to cook so dice them very finely before adding to the soup with the other vegetables. A pinch of smoky Spanish paprika will add a slightly different flavour.

This version of a minestrone is really a meal in its own right. It's packed with lovely winter vegetables and is a 'one-pot wonder' that will only improve with age.

chunky chickpea soup

2 tablespoons olive oil

1 leek, thinly sliced

1 small fennel bulb, cut into small dice

100 g pancetta, cut into small cubes

1 carrot, grated

1 potato, cut into small dice

1.5 litres chicken stock

400 g canned chickpeas, drained and rinsed

80 g spinach, chopped

salt and black pepper

50 g Parmesan cheese, grated, to serve

serves 4

Heat the oil in a saucepan. Add the leek, fennel and pancetta and cook for 5 minutes over high heat, until the leek softens and the pancetta really flavours the oil. Add the carrot, potato, stock and chickpeas and bring to the boil.

Reduce the heat and simmer for 20 minutes. Season to taste then add the spinach. Cook over low heat for 5 minutes, until the spinach has wilted throughout the soup.

Serve with Parmesan sprinkled over the top.

Variation Add 100 g small pasta (try the little rice-shaped pastas such as risoni or orzo) instead of chickpeas and simmer until the pasta is cooked through before adding the final few ingredients.

Orange or red lentils work best for this recipe as they are quick to soften and also help to create the rich autumnal colour. You can forgo the bread and goats' cheese if you want to make this dish lighter but it does add a certain depth to the soup.

carrot & lentil soup

3 tablespoons butter

1 red onion, chopped

1 garlic clove, chopped

2 tablespoons sun-dried tomato purée

500 g carrots, grated

250 g red lentils, rinsed and drained

1.5 litres chicken stock

4 slices of rye bread

50 g soft goats' cheese

serves 4

Heat the butter in a heavy-based saucepan over high heat. When the butter is sizzling, add the onion and garlic and cook for 4–5 minutes, stirring often. Add the sun-dried tomato purée and stir-fry for 1 minute. Add the carrots, lentils and stock to the pan. Bring to the boil and cook at a rapid simmer for 40 minutes, until the lentils are soft.

Spoon the soup, in batches, into a blender and process until smooth. Return the soup to the saucepan and cook over low heat for a few minutes, until heated through.

Toast the rye bread and, while it's still warm, spread over the cheese. Float the toast on top of the soup to serve.

Puy lentils, grown in France, are great at thickening soups without turning sludgy. They give this soup a pert little bite which is offset by the soft, buttery vegetables and enriched by the heady tang of the dried oregano. It makes a great winter warmer.

Puy lentil & vegetable soup

50 g butter

2 carrots, peeled and finely chopped

2 leeks, white part only, thinly sliced

1 onion, finely chopped

3 garlic cloves, sliced

½ teaspoon dried chilli flakes

2 teaspoons dried oregano

400 g canned chopped plum tomatoes

200 g Puy lentils

1 litre vegetable stock

freshly grated pecorino or Parmesan cheese, to serve

salt and black pepper

serves 4–6

Melt the butter in a heavy-based saucepan. Add the carrots, leeks, onion and garlic and a large pinch of salt. Stir until everything is coated in butter and cook over medium heat, with the lid on, for 15 minutes, stirring occasionally.

Once the vegetables have softened, add the chilli flakes, oregano, tomatoes, lentils and stock. Cover again and leave to simmer for 30 minutes, or until the lentils are cooked. Season to taste.

Transfer to bowls and serve with buttered toast and grated pecorino or Parmesan cheese on the side.

Coconut milk and Puy lentils make perfect companions. If you can't get hold of any Puy lentils, use green or brown ones. Add the spinach at the end: it doesn't need cooking. This soup is full of rich flavours – you would never guess that it's vegan.

lentil, coconut & wilted spinach soup

150 g Puy lentils

1 litre vegetable stock

1 onion, chopped

2 garlic cloves, chopped

2 teaspoons ground cumin

250 ml canned coconut milk or 100 g creamed coconut, chopped and dissolved in 150 ml boiling water

4 small handfuls of baby spinach, about 50 g

salt and black pepper

serves 4

Rinse the lentils, then put in a large saucepan and add enough cold water just to cover. Boil for 10 minutes, then add the remaining ingredients, except the spinach. Reduce the heat and simmer for 20–30 minutes or until the lentils are tender.

Put a small handful of the spinach in 4 bowls and ladle the soup on top. The heat from the soup will wilt the leaves.

Roasting is the best way to use tomatoes when they are not quite ripe, or so mass produced as to be flavourless. They go extremely well with lentils and they look good too. Lentils don't require soaking, so after the vegetables have been charred, this becomes a very quick soup to make.

lentil & roasted tomato soup

6 tomatoes, about 500 g, cut into wedges

1 large onion, thickly sliced

3 tablespoons olive oil

a few sprigs of fresh herbs, such as thyme, sage or oregano (or 1 tablespoon dried mixed herbs)

2 large celery sticks, chopped

1 large carrot, diced

4 garlic cloves, sliced

1 litre chicken stock

200 g Puy lentils or other green lentils

1 fresh bay leaf

50 g baby spinach leaves

a handful of chopped fresh flat leaf parsley

salt and black pepper

serves 4–6

Preheat the oven to 220°C (425°F) Gas 7.

Put the tomatoes, onion and 2 tablespoons of the oil in a baking dish. Toss well and spread to an even layer. Strip the leaves off the herb sprigs and sprinkle over the top. Add a good pinch of salt and roast in the preheated oven until charred, 20–25 minutes.

Meanwhile, to prepare the lentils, put the remaining 1 tablespoon oil in a large saucepan over medium high heat. Add the celery, carrot and garlic and cook until just brown and beginning to smell aromatic. Add the stock and 600 ml water. Stir in the lentils, bay leaf and a good pinch of salt. Bring to the boil, then lower the heat, cover and simmer gently until the lentils are tender, 15–20 minutes.

Coarsely chop the roasted tomatoes and onions and add to the lentil soup. Season to taste. Stir in the spinach and parsley and serve.

Variation Towards the end of the cooking time, add some cooked chorizo or Italian sausage to make this a more substantial dish.

This is Lebanese in origin, but soups like this are served all over the Middle East. Crispy fried onions are a lovely topping, but you have to be brave and really brown them so they look almost black. Make sure you really soften them to start with.

lentil, spinach & cumin soup

3 tablespoons olive oil

2 onions, chopped

4 garlic cloves, chopped

1 teaspoon ground coriander

1 teaspoon cumin seeds

150 g brown or green lentils

1.25 litres vegetable stock

200 g spinach

juice of 1 lemon

salt and black pepper

to serve

4 tablespoons Greek yoghurt

25 g pine nuts, lightly toasted

serves 4

Heat the olive oil in a large, heavy-based saucepan and add the onions. Cook, covered, for 8–10 minutes until softened. Remove half the onion and set aside.

Continue to cook the onion left in the pan for a further 10 minutes until deep brown, sweet and caramelized. Take out and set aside for the garnish.

Return the softened onion to the pan and add the garlic, coriander, cumin seeds and lentils and stir for 1–2 minutes until well coated in oil. Add the stock, bring to the boil, then turn down to a gentle simmer for 30 minutes until the lentils are lovely and soft.

Add the spinach and stir until wilted. Transfer half the soup to a blender and liquidize until you have a purée. Stir back into the soup. Season with lemon juice, salt and black pepper.

Divide the soup between 4 bowls, add a dollop of Greek yoghurt and scatter the pine nuts and fried onions over the top.

This hearty Scandinavian soup often has no meat in it, using celeriac instead. If you fancy making a vegetarian version, halve your celeriac, peel it and cut into cubes, adding it at the same time as the peas. If you can't find yellow split peas in your supermarket, try an Indian one and buy yellow channa dhaal.

Swedish yellow pea soup

1 smoked pork knuckle or ham hock

500 g yellow split peas

2 onions, halved lengthways

6 cloves, stuck in the onions

1 carrot, chopped

3 fresh bay leaves

3 long curls of orange zest

4 tablespoons Dijon mustard

salt and black pepper

snipped fresh chives, to serve

serves 4

Put the pork knuckle in a snug-fitting saucepan and cover it with cold water. Bring to the boil, reduce the heat and simmer until tender. Skim it from time to time and top up with more boiling water as necessary. When done, the meat will fall easily off the bone. Drain, remove the skin and bone and pull the meat into bite-sized shreds. Reserve 250 ml of the cooking liquid.

Rinse the peas and put in a large saucepan. Add the onions stuck with cloves, the carrot, bay leaves, orange zest and 1 litre water. Bring to the boil, reduce the heat and simmer until done, about 30 minutes.

The peas should be soft, but still keep their shape. If not, cook for 5–10 minutes more. Remove the cloves, bay leaves, orange zest and (optional) the onions and carrot.

Stir in the mustard and pork shreds and taste for seasoning. Instead of salt, use some of the reserved liquid from cooking the pork. It will be salty and meaty – take care, it's easy to add too much. Ladle into 4 bowls and serve sprinkled with the chives.

meat & poultry

On a hot summer's day, a chilled soup makes for a perfect lunch. The serrano ham adds a salty kick and makes this soup a little more substantial than it would be otherwise.

chilled melon soup with serrano ham

4 cantaloupe melons

6 spring onions, finely chopped

2 tablespoons chopped fresh basil

1 tablespoon stem ginger syrup

300 ml plain yoghurt

2 tablespoons dry sherry

2 large slices serrano or Parma ham

salt and black pepper

ice cubes, to serve

serves 4

Cut the melons in half and discard the seeds. Scoop out all the flesh and transfer it to a blender. Add the spring onions and basil and blend until smooth.

Add the ginger syrup, yoghurt and sherry, blend until very smooth and season to taste. Chill for about 1 hour.

Cook the ham under a preheated grill until very crisp and golden. Let cool and break up into bite sized pieces.

Pour the soup into chilled bowls, add a few ice cubes, a sprinkling of ham and a good grinding of black pepper, then serve.

A chowder normally contains fish and is reputed to have come from the large cauldrons found on fishermen's boats called *chaudières*. Somehow sweetcorn replaced the fish over in New England, but the principle is still the same – a creamy stock thickened with potatoes and spiked with the rich flavour of smoky bacon.

sweetcorn & pancetta chowder

40 g butter

150 g pancetta, cubed

1 onion, sliced

2 carrots, finely chopped

300 g new potatoes (unpeeled), thinly sliced

2 tablespoons plain flour

600 ml whole milk

400 ml chicken or vegetable stock

3 dried bay leaves

300 g sweetcorn (thawed if frozen)

3 tablespoons double cream

salt and black pepper

serves 4

Heat the butter in a large saucepan and fry the pancetta until crisp. Add the onion, carrots and potatoes, cover and cook on medium/low heat for 15–20 minutes until soft. Stir occasionally.

Sprinkle the flour into the pan and cook for 1 minute, stirring it into the vegetables. Pour in the milk gradually, blending it with the flour, then add the stock and bay leaves; bring to a gentle simmer. Add the sweetcorn and cook for 5 minutes.

Remove from the heat, discard the bay leaves, stir in the cream and season with salt.

Divide the soup between 4 bowls and serve with a fresh grinding of black pepper.

Children love alphabet pasta. It can be added to all sorts of soups, but is especially useful with vegetable soups, to encourage the little critters to eat their greens. If you want to make this vegetarian, omit the pancetta and use vegetable rather than chicken stock.

alphabet soup

100 g pancetta, cubed

1 tablespoon olive oil

½ onion, chopped

1 large potato, diced

1 carrot, chopped

2 celery sticks, sliced

2 small courgettes, chopped

3 tomatoes, chopped

1 litre chicken stock

500 g alfabetto soup pasta

½ small cabbage, sliced

100 g green beans, chopped

100 g peas, fresh or frozen

200 g canned beans, such as cannellini, drained and rinsed

salt and black pepper

2 tablespoons chopped fresh flat leaf parsley, to serve

serves 4

Put the pancetta in a frying pan, heat gently and fry until the fat runs. Add the oil, heat briefly, then add the onion and cook gently until softened but not browned.

Add the potato, carrot, celery, courgettes, tomatoes and salt and pepper. Add the stock and the pasta and heat until simmering. Cook over low heat for about 15 minutes. Add the cabbage and beans, bring to the boil and cook for 5 minutes, then add the peas and canned beans and cook for another 2–3 minutes until all the vegetables are tender. Add salt and pepper to taste then divide between 4 bowls and serve sprinkled with parsley and some bread on the side, if you like.

This recipe is inspired by a Polish soup called *zurek*. Oatmeal is used to thicken the soup rather than the traditional ingredient of fermented flour batter. It's a wonderfully hearty number.

bacon & Savoy cabbage soup

2 tablespoons olive oil

8 rashers of smoked, streaky bacon, sliced

1 onion, chopped

2 garlic cloves, crushed

a pinch of ground allspice

300 g potatoes, peeled and diced

¼ Savoy cabbage, shredded

400 ml chicken stock

400 ml whole milk

2 tablespoons fine oatmeal

black pepper

serves 4

Heat the oil in a heavy-based saucepan and fry the bacon for 2–3 minutes, until cooked. Turn the heat down and add the onion and garlic. Cover and cook for 3 minutes or until starting to soften.

Add the allspice and potatoes, cover and cook for a further 2–3 minutes to start softening the potatoes. Add the cabbage and stir until it has wilted into the rest of the ingredients. Pour in the stock and milk and bring to the boil.

Mix the oatmeal with 3–4 tablespoons cold water until smooth and gradually whisk into the soup to thicken.

Divide the soup between 4 bowls and serve with a fresh grinding of black pepper.

This warming soup will bring sunshine to a winter's day. If you cannot find cajun spice blend, it's easy to make your own from white, black and cayenne pepper, along with celery salt.

cajun-spiced chowder with corn & bacon

4 corn-on-the-cob or 475 g fresh or frozen kernels

25 g butter

1 onion, finely chopped

1 celery stick, finely chopped

4–5 slices back bacon, chopped

1½ teaspoons Cajun spice blend, plus extra to serve

1.25 litres vegetable stock

250 ml single cream

2 tablespoons chopped fresh oregano, to serve

an extra pinch of Cajun spice blend

serves 4

If using fresh corn cobs, remove the husks and silks and cut the stalk end flat. Put the flat end on a board and cut off the kernels from top to bottom. Discard the cobs.

Melt the butter in a large saucepan, add the onion and fry for 5 minutes. Add the celery and fry for a further 3 minutes until well softened. Add the bacon and cook for 1–2 minutes. Add the corn and Cajun spice blend and mix well.

Add the stock and bring to the boil. Reduce the heat and simmer for 35 minutes. Add the cream and simmer until thickened. You can serve the soup immediately, or, to thicken it further, put a ladle of the chowder (without any of the bacon) into a blender and purée until smooth. Pour the blended chowder back into the pan and mix well.

To serve, ladle into bowls and top with a little oregano and a very light dusting of Cajun spice blend.

This soup is salty, sweet, meaty and sour all at once. Brisket of beef is perfect for this dish as it cooks down to meltingly tender flakes of deliciousness. All that red meat and stock is quite heavy and it needs the fresh herbs to perk up all the flavours. So just bear in mind that the garnish is not a frilly afterthought, but integral to the dish.

beef & sweet potato soup

3 garlic cloves, peeled

2 shallots, chopped

2 green chillies, deseeded and chopped

450 g beef brisket

2 tablespoons groundnut oil

1.5 litres hot beef stock

4 tablespoons tamarind paste

4 kaffir lime leaves

2 sweet potatoes, peeled and cut into 2-cm chunks

1 tablespoon clear honey

sea salt

to serve

a handful of fresh mint and coriander leaves

2 shallots, sliced

1 red chilli, deseeded and sliced

serves 4

Using a pestle and mortar, pound together the garlic, shallots and chillies to make a paste.

Blanch the beef in a pan of boiling water for 1 minute, then drain. Rinse the beef to get rid of any impurities, then thinly slice.

Heat the oil in a heavy-based saucepan, then add the beef and brown evenly. Add the spice paste and toss for 1–2 minutes until fragrant, but don't allow it to burn. Add the beef stock, tamarind paste and lime leaves and simmer for 2 hours until the beef is really tender.

Add the sweet potatoes and simmer for a further 30 minutes until tender. Season with honey and sea salt to taste.

Divide the soup between 4 bowls. Serve with the plate of fresh herbs, shallots and red chilli so everyone can season to taste.

From the land that brings us haggis, neeps and tatties comes its famous namesake broth. This version veers from the traditional with its inclusion of brown rice and soy sauce. You can add extra herbs if you like – thyme, in particular, likes being with lamb.

Scotch broth

2 tablespoons olive oil

1 carrot, chopped

1 leek, chopped

2 celery sticks, diced and leaves chopped

500 g stewing lamb, well trimmed of fat and cubed

500 ml chicken stock

1 tablespoon light soy sauce

100 g brown rice

salt and black pepper

serves 4

Heat the oil in a large saucepan. Add the carrot, leek, celery sticks and leaves and cook over high heat for 5 minutes, stirring often. Add the lamb, stock, soy sauce, rice and 1 litre of water. Bring to the boil.

Reduce the heat to low, cover with a tight-fitting lid and let the soup simmer for 1 hour. Season to taste and serve.

This is Vietnamese fast food – it's slurped down in a flash but be warned that it takes time to make. It's pronounced 'fuh' and derives from the French *pot au feu* ('pot on fire'). It's a soothing, deeply flavoured broth bobbing with beef and rice noodles, served with a bowl of Thai basil, mint and chilli which you add to taste.

Vietnamese beef pho

1 tablespoon sunflower oil

1 star anise

1 cinnamon stick

1 tablespoon coriander seeds

3 cm fresh ginger, sliced

4 garlic cloves

1.5 litres beef stock

3 sprigs of fresh coriander

150 g rice noodles

4 tablespoons lime juice

2 tablespoons fish sauce

200 g sirloin steak, thinly sliced

100 g beansprouts

to serve

10 g fresh Thai basil leaves

5 g fresh mint leaves

1 red chilli, sliced

serves 4

Heat the oil in a large saucepan over low heat, then add the anise, cinnamon, coriander seeds, ginger and garlic. Cook gently for 1–2 minutes to release their aromas. Add the stock and bring to the boil.

Add the coriander sprigs and simmer for 30 minutes. Take off the heat and leave to infuse while you prepare the other ingredients.

Pile up the Thai basil, mint and chilli on a plate and keep in the fridge until you're ready.

When you're ready to eat, cook the rice noodles in a large pan of boiling water according to the manufacturer's instructions. Drain and refresh under cold running water. Divide between 4 bowls.

Strain the stock back into the pan and add enough lime juice and fish sauce to taste. Add the beef and cook for 1 minute, or until it is just cooked through. Ladle the beef and stock onto the noodles and scatter the beansprouts over the top. Serve with the plate of condiments so everyone can season to taste.

Do not despair at the thought of making wontons – you can actually buy wonton 'skins' either chilled or frozen in Chinese supermarkets. In fact, this is a speedy soup to make and highly virtuous too. You can substitute the chicken for pork fillet if you prefer.

wonton chicken soup

8 Chinese cabbage leaves

1 carrot, chopped

1 cooked chicken breast, shredded

2 spring onions, finely sliced

a handful of beansprouts

wontons

125 g chicken breast, sliced

3 spring onions, chopped

a pinch of salt

1 teaspoon grated fresh ginger

2 cans water chestnuts

1 egg white, lightly beaten

12 small wonton wrappers

chinese chicken stock

1.5 litres chicken stock

4 star anise

5 cm fresh ginger, sliced

serves 4

Bring a large saucepan of water to the boil. Add the Chinese cabbage leaves and carrot and blanch for 1 minute. Set aside the carrot and plunge the cabbage into a bowl of iced water for 5 minutes. Drain. Cut out and discard the white ribs. Put 4 leaves, one on top of the other, on a tea towel. Roll them up into a cylinder and press out the liquid. Cut the cylinder crossways into 3 cm long sections. Repeat with the other 4 leaves, to make cabbage 'sushi'.

To make the wontons, put the chicken in a food processor and pulse until minced. Add the spring onions, salt and ginger and pulse again. Transfer to a bowl and stir in the water chestnuts. Brush a circle of egg white around the centre of each wonton wrapper and put 1 teaspoon of mixture in the middle. Twirl the wrapper around the filling to make a shuttlecock shape. Press to seal.

Put the stock ingredients in a saucepan and simmer for 10 minutes. Strain to remove the flavourings, then return the stock to the rinsed pan. Reheat the stock, add the wontons and poach them for 1½ minutes – they will rise to the surface like fresh pasta (which is what they are). Divide the wontons, stock, chicken, cabbage and carrot between bowls, top with the spring onions and beansprouts and serve.

Laksas are spicy soups from Malaysia, Indonesia and the Philippines, though the Malay ones are the best known. They contain vegetables, prawns, pork and noodles, though this varies from region to region. This one contains chicken, but do feel free to substitute it for fish and other seafood instead.

laksa

3 tablespoons groundnut oil

500 ml canned coconut milk

2 skinless chicken breasts

fish sauce

100 g fresh udon noodles

1 packet beansprouts

4 spring onions, sliced

1 red chilli, finely sliced

sprigs of fresh coriander

spice paste

3–6 red chillies, chopped

1 shallot, chopped

2 lemongrass stalks, sliced

3 cm fresh ginger, sliced

½ teaspoon ground turmeric

6 blanched almonds, chopped

1 tablespoon fish sauce

serves 4

Put all the spice paste ingredients into a spice grinder or blender and work to a paste (add a little water if necessary).

Heat the oil in a wok, add the spice paste and cook gently for about 5 minutes until aromatic. Add the thick part of the coconut milk (if any) and stir-fry until it throws out its oil, then add the thinner part and heat gently. Add 1 litre water and bring to the boil. Slice the chicken and add to the wok. Reduce the heat and poach gently without boiling until the chicken is cooked through, about 10–15 minutes. Add fish sauce to taste.

Rinse the noodles in cold water, then boil for 1–2 minutes. Divide the noodles between large soup bowls. Add the chicken and liquid, top with the beansprouts, spring onions, chilli, garlic and coriander and serve immediately.

This classic Greek recipe is great for using up leftover cooked chicken. The idea of eating soup with egg and lemon juice may sound unusual but it works. In Greece, soup is regarded as a main course with family members having second or even third helpings.

chicken avgolemono

1.4 litres chicken stock

100 g long-grain rice

400 g cooked chicken, shredded

3 eggs

juice of 1 lemon

fried garlic croutons

100 ml olive oil

3 slices of stale white bread, 2 cm thick, cut into 2-cm cubes

4 whole garlic cloves, unpeeled

chopped fresh flat leaf parsley, to serve

serves 4

To make the croutons, heat the oil in a frying pan until a bread cube sizzles and turns brown in 4 seconds. Add the bread and garlic. Cook, stirring constantly, over medium heat for 2 minutes, or until golden brown. Discard the garlic and drain the croutons on kitchen paper.

Heat the stock in a large saucepan and add the rice. Bring to the boil and simmer for 15 minutes or until the rice is tender. Add the chicken and warm through for 2–3 minutes.

In the meantime, whisk the eggs with the lemon juice in a small bowl. Add a ladleful of the warm stock and whisk until thinned. Remove the soup from the heat and gradually pour in the egg mixture, whisking to amalgamate it. It should thicken in the residual heat, but if you need to, place it over low heat for just 3–4 minutes, stirring the bottom of the pan to thicken. Do not return to high heat once the egg has been added, or it will boil and scramble.

Divide the soup between 4 bowls and garnish with parsley and Fried Garlic Croutons.

This aromatic broth is a hit with children and will warm the family up on a winter's evening. It's low in fat too. If you can't find Jewish egg noodles, substitute them with vermicelli.

chicken noodle soup

2 tablespoons olive oil

1.4 kg chicken drumsticks and thighs

1 onion, chopped

1 carrot, peeled and chopped

1 garlic clove, sliced

2 celery sticks, chopped

1 bouquet garni (fresh bay leaf, thyme and parsley)

1 onion, chopped

2 carrots, chopped

2 celery sticks, chopped

20 g chopped fresh flat leaf parsley

90 g fine Jewish egg noodles, broken into pieces

salt and pepper

serves 4

Heat 1 tablespoon of the oil in a large, heavy-based saucepan. Season the chicken pieces and brown them in the pan in batches. Put all the chicken pieces back in the pot with the onion, carrot, garlic and celery, and cook over low heat for 15 minutes. Pour in 1.5 litres water, add the bouquet garni and simmer, covered, for 1 hour over medium/low heat. Remove any foamy scum from the surface during cooking.

Strain the finished stock through a fine sieve into a bowl and skim off any excess fat. Reserve the chicken and let cool before removing the meat from the bones and roughly chopping it.

Heat the remaining olive oil in a saucepan. Add the onion, carrots and celery, and season. Fry for 5 minutes, then pour in the stock. Bring to the boil and add the noodles. Cook until the noodles are al dente, then add the chopped chicken. Sprinkle in the parsley, stir and serve.

The chicken stock that forms the basis of this tasty soup is packed with flavours of Asia to give it a wonderful punch. The stock does take a bit of preparation but it's well worth it.

chicken & vegetable soup

a handful of asparagus tips

a large handful of sugar snap peas, cut into 2–3 pieces each

1 punnet cherry tomatoes, quartered and deseeded

salt and black pepper

chicken stock

1 small organic chicken

2 whole star anise

2 cinnamon sticks

a handful of kaffir lime leaves

2 lemongrass stalks, sliced

7 cm fresh ginger, sliced

4 whole garlic cloves

1 red chilli, halved lengthways

1 tablespoon black peppercorns

fresh coriander or parsley, to serve

serves 4

To make the stock, put all the ingredients in a large saucepan, add water to cover the chicken by 3 cm, bring to the boil, reduce the heat and simmer for at least 1 hour.

Remove the chicken, whole, from the pan and reserve. Scoop out the solids from the stock, reserving the ginger. Put the ginger on a plate and cut into tiny slivers.

Strain the stock into a saucepan, ladling at first, then pouring through muslin. It should be clear but slightly fatty on top. Season to taste.

Pull shreds of chicken off the bird and cut into bite-sized pieces if necessary. Leave to one side, covered.

Return the stock to the boil, add the ginger slivers and the asparagus and blanch for 30 seconds. Add the sugar snap peas, tomato quarters and chicken and blanch for 30 seconds. You are heating them and keeping the peas and tomatoes fresh, rather than cooking them to a mush. Ladle into large soup bowls and top with the herb of your choice.

This rice soup is sustaining enough to serve as a main, and the ginger makes it great for fighting off a cold. It's wonderfully aromatic. You can switch the chicken for prawns if you prefer.

chicken, ginger & rice soup

50 g basmati rice

500 ml chicken stock

1½ tablespoons light soy sauce

½ teaspoon dried chilli flakes

½ lemongrass stalk, outer leaves removed, finely chopped

3 cm fresh ginger, sliced

2 garlic cloves, thinly sliced

3 chicken breasts (each about 150 g), cut into small pieces

1 red pepper, cored, deseeded and thinly sliced

3 spring onions, finely chopped

50 g Chinese cabbage, finely shredded (optional)

a squeeze of lime juice

black pepper

fresh coriander leaves, to garnish

serves 2–4

Cook the rice according to the packet instructions. Drain, rinse, drain again and set aside until needed.

Heat the stock to boiling point in a large pan. Add the soy sauce, chilli flakes, lemongrass, ginger and garlic, and cook over high heat for 5 minutes.

Add the chicken pieces and red pepper and let the mixture gently bubble for about 3 minutes, or until the chicken is tender.

Add the cooked rice and cook for a further 1 minute. Finally, stir in the spring onions and cabbage (if using). Ladle into warmed bowls. Squeeze a little lime juice over each, season with pepper and garnish with coriander leaves. Serve immediately.

Variation This soup also works well using shelled uncooked prawns. Simply substitute them for the chicken and cook in the same way. Add a handful of spinach leaves at the end.

Summer sweetcorn, bursting with flavour and sweetness, is the main ingredient here, subtly enhanced with fresh ginger. When used with spring onions as it is here, ginger brings balance to a dish.

sweetcorn & chicken soup

1 chicken breast (about 250 g), cut into 2-cm cubes

1 tablespoon cornflour

1 tablespoon light soy sauce

1 tablespoon Chinese rice wine (or dry sherry)

1 tablespoon vegetable oil

2 teaspoons grated fresh ginger

2 spring onions, thinly sliced

1 leek, thinly sliced

1 celery stick, thinly sliced

2 corn-on-the-cobs, kernels shucked

2 litres chicken stock

½ teaspoon salt

½ teaspoon sugar

½ teaspoon white pepper

a large handful of chopped fresh coriander

serves 4

Put the chicken, cornflour, soy sauce and rice wine in a bowl and stir well. Cover and refrigerate for 1 hour.

Heat the oil in a saucepan over high heat and cook the ginger, spring onions, leek and celery for 2–3 minutes, until softened but not brown.

Add the sweetcorn kernels and cook for 1 minute. Add the stock and the salt, sugar and white pepper and bring to the boil. Reduce the heat to a low simmer and cook for 10 minutes.

Add the chicken and marinade to the soup, stirring to separate the chicken pieces, cover and cook for 5 minutes, until it is cooked.

Divide the coriander between 4 bowls and ladle the soup over to serve.

Variation This light soup can be made more substantial and hearty with the addition of lightly beaten egg. Whisk 2 eggs in a bowl until just combined and slowly pour them into the simmering soup in a steady stream. Using a chopstick, gently stir for an authentic-looking Chinese soup.

This soup carries all the flavours of south India. The tempered topping may seem a little fiddly but it is worth the effort. The addition of rice makes this substantial enough for a light supper.

Goan chicken soup

1 tablespoon groundnut oil

1 onion, finely chopped

3 garlic cloves, crushed

3 cm fresh ginger, grated

125 g rice, preferably basmati

½ teaspoon ground turmeric

1 litre chicken stock

100 g shelled green peas

500 g cooked chicken, shredded

salt and black pepper

tempered topping

2 tablespoons groundnut oil

1 tablespoon mustard seeds

2–4 garlic cloves, finely sliced

3 small white onions, finely sliced

a handful of curry leaves (optional)

serves 4

Heat the oil in a saucepan, add the onion, garlic and ginger and fry gently until softened but not browned. Add the rice, turmeric, salt and pepper and stock.

Simmer for 10 minutes, then add the peas and chicken and simmer until the rice is soft, about another 10 minutes.

To make the tempered topping, a favourite garnish in India, heat the oil in a wok or frying pan, add the mustard seeds and fry until they pop. Add the garlic and stir-fry until crisp. Take care, because it can easily burn and burned garlic is bitter. Remove with a slotted spoon and set aside. Add the onions and stir-fry at a low temperature until well covered with oil. Continue cooking until tender. Add the curry leaves, if using, and cook for a few minutes until aromatic. Return the garlic to the mixture and remove from the heat.

Ladle the soup into bowls, top with the tempered mixture and serve.

Any number of vegetables may be added to this chicken noodle soup. Enoki mushrooms with their clumps of long stalks work particularly well and are available to buy in many supermarkets but can be substituted for shiitake mushrooms.

Indonesian chicken soup

1.5 litres chicken stock

500 g chicken pieces, skinless

1 carrot, finely sliced

300 g dried rice noodles

2–3 tablespoons groundnut oil

1 onion, finely sliced

1–2 bunches enoki mushrooms,

1 baby courgette, finely sliced

4 spring onions, finely sliced

2–4 green chillies, finely sliced

2 limes, cut into wedges

spice paste

2 lemongrass stalks

2 tablespoons black pepper

2 tablespoons fish sauce

2 teaspoons ground turmeric

2 small onions, finely chopped

3 cm fresh ginger, grated

6 garlic cloves, crushed

125 g blanched almonds

serves 4

Bring the stock to the boil, add the chicken, reduce the heat and poach gently until tender. Remove from the stock to a plate, let cool slightly, then shred. Return the stock to the boil, add the carrot and simmer until tender. Remove the carrot and add to the chicken. Set the stock aside and keep it warm.

Put the noodles in a bowl and cover with hot water. Let soak for about 15 minutes, then drain and keep in cold water until ready to serve.

To make the spice paste, cut the top off the lemongrass, keeping the white part only. Remove and discard the 2 outer leaves, and finely slice the rest. Put in a small blender, then add the rest of the spice paste ingredients and blend until you get a coarse texture. Set aside. You will use about 2 tablespoons for this recipe – freeze the rest in ice cube trays for future use.

Heat 2 tablespoons of the oil in a wok, add the sliced onion and fry until crispy. Remove with a slotted spoon and drain on kitchen paper.

Reheat the oil, adding an extra tablespoon if necessary, then add the spice paste and fry gently until fragrant. Add the chicken and carrots, and stir-fry briefly to cover with the spices. Add the stock, mushrooms and courgette and heat until very hot – this will blanch the vegetables. Drain the noodles and divide between 4 bowls. Ladle the chicken, vegetables and stock over the noodles and serve, topped with the spring onions, fried onions and half the chillies. Serve lime or lemon wedges and remaining chillies in separate dishes.

This soup is utterly delicious. If you've had a roast it's a good way of using up those last little bits of meat. There's nothing more satisfyingly thrifty than getting two meals from one bird.

roast chicken, garlic & watercress soup

a whole chicken (1.2 kg)

3 whole garlic bulbs

1 baking potato (300 g)

2 tablespoons extra virgin olive oil, plus extra to serve

6 sprigs of fresh thyme

900 ml chicken stock

150 g watercress

salt and black pepper

serves 4

Preheat the oven to 200°C (400°F) Gas 6.

Place the chicken in a roasting tray, wrap the garlic bulbs and potato in foil individually and scatter around the edges. Drizzle the oil over the chicken, scatter the thyme sprigs over the top and season well. Roast in the preheated oven for 1 hour.

Open the packages of roasted garlic and potato to allow them to cool off and at the same time check that they are really soft inside. If not, return to the oven for a little longer until soft. Pull the chicken meat from the carcass and keep the carcass for making chicken stock.

Pour the stock into a large saucepan. Discard the skin from the potato, chop and add it to the pan. Cut the tops off the garlic bulbs, squeeze out the soft flesh from inside the cloves and add to the soup.

Chop up the chicken meat and add that to the soup too. Transfer about a third of the soup to a blender along with the watercress and liquidize until smooth. Return to the pan and stir until blended. Add more water if you think it's too thick. Season to taste.

Divide the soup between 4 bowls and drizzle with extra oil.

This is a classic Thai soup called *Tom Ka Gai*. It shouldn't sting the senses with chilli, which is how some restaurants make it. You can serve it without the rice noodles as a starter.

Thai chicken & coconut soup

125 g rice noodles

400 ml coconut milk

200 ml chicken stock

2 lemongrass stalks, halved lengthways and bruised

5 cm fresh ginger, sliced

5 kaffir lime leaves

3 tablespoons demerara sugar

2 tablespoons fish sauce

3 red chillies, bruised

200 g chicken breast or thigh, skinless and sliced into 2-cm strips

150 g oyster mushrooms, halved

juice of 1–2 limes

fresh coriander leaves, to serve

serves 4

Put the noodles in a bowl and cover with boiling water. Leave to soak for 15 minutes while you make the rest of the soup.

Put the coconut milk, stock, lemongrass, ginger and lime leaves in a large saucepan and slowly bring to the boil over medium heat. Add the sugar, fish sauce, chillies, chicken and mushrooms and simmer for 6–8 minutes until the chicken is cooked through.

Stir in the lime juice and taste. If it needs more salt, add a dash of fish sauce and if it is hot and salty, it may need rounding off with a touch more sugar.

Drain the noodles and divide between 4 bowls. Ladle the soup over the noodles, garnish with the coriander and serve.

You can opt for a supermarket curry paste or buy it fresh from a Thai shop, where you can also pick up the Thai yellow egg-shaped aubergines, which are used in this recipe for their bitter taste.

duck soup

4 tablespoons groundnut oil

1–2 skinless duck breasts

150 g dried wide rice stick noodles (optional)

3 egg-shaped yellow, white or purple aubergines, or small Chinese aubergines, quartered and deseeded (optional)

2–4 tablespoons Thai red curry paste

1 teaspoon sugar

2 tablespoons fish sauce, or to taste

1 litre chicken stock

250 g green beans

to serve

2–3 limes, cut into wedges

chopped chillies

serves 4

To prepare the duck breasts, preheat a wok, add 2 tablespoons of the oil and sear the duck breasts on all sides. You are just sealing the outside – the inside should be raw. Remove, cool and freeze. Just before cooking, slice them very finely.

Soak the noodles, if using, in hot water for 15 minutes. Boil for 1–2 minutes, then drain and plunge into cold water.

Add the remaining oil to the wok, add the aubergine, if using, and stir-fry until browned on the edges and softened. Remove and set aside.

Add the curry paste to the wok and stir-fry gently to release the aromas. Add the sugar and stir-fry for a minute or so. Add 1 teaspoon of the fish sauce and stir-fry again. Add the stock and bring to the boil. Add the aubergines, if using, and the beans. Return to the boil and simmer for 15 minutes. Taste, add extra fish sauce as needed and set aside for 15 minutes.

When ready to serve, reheat the vegetables and stock, add the duck slices and cook for 1 minute. Drain the noodles, cover with boiling water, then drain again.

Divide the noodles and stock mixture between large bowls and serve with extra lime wedges and a dish of chopped chillies.

This soup is sold all over Morocco. It varies according to the region but usually contains a little meat, tomatoes and lots of spices. Harrira is served as an important part of the festivities of Ramadan – it's traditionally used to break the fast and is substantial enough to be considered a meal in itself.

harrira

2 tablespoons olive oil

1 lamb shank (475 g)

2 onions, sliced

3 celery sticks, chopped

3 garlic cloves, chopped

1 teaspoon ground cinnamon

½ teaspoon saffron threads

½ teaspoon ground ginger

several gratings of nutmeg

1 tablespoon tomato purée

4 tomatoes, chopped

700 ml lamb stock or water

200 g canned chickpeas, rinsed and drained

100 g green lentils, rinsed

juice of 1 lemon

2 tablespoons chopped fresh coriander

salt and black pepper

serves 4–6

Heat the oil in a heavy-based saucepan, then add the lamb and brown evenly. Add the onions, celery, garlic, cinnamon, saffron, ginger and nutmeg and season well. Turn the heat down a little, cover and cook for 10 minutes until soft, stirring occasionally.

Stir in the tomato purée and the tomatoes and cook for a further 2–3 minutes. Add the stock, cover and cook for 1 hour until the lamb is becoming tender.

Add the chickpeas and lentils and cook for a further 40 minutes until they are tender and the lamb can easily be pulled off the bone. Shred the meat from the shank, remove the bone and discard. Add lemon juice to taste and check the seasoning (it needs quite a generous amount of salt). Stir in the coriander.

Divide the soup between 4–6 bowls and tuck in.

This brothy soup filled with meatballs and rice is wonderfully comforting. The fresh herbs and ginger give it a light flavour. If you like, you can make the meatballs ahead of the soup.

Thai pork & rice soup

meatballs

3 garlic cloves, chopped

10 g fresh coriander

450 g minced pork

2 teaspoons fish sauce

¼ teaspoon white pepper

soup

1.25 litres chicken stock

2 cm fresh ginger, sliced

1 teaspoon sugar

1 tablespoon fish sauce

100 g Chinese cabbage, shredded

100 g cooked short-grain rice or 150 g rice stick noodles

to serve

6 spring onions, shredded

½ teaspoon sesame oil

serves 4

To make the meatballs, put the garlic and coriander in a food processor and blend together until chopped. Add the pork, fish sauce and pepper and process. Wet your hands and roll the mixture into 2-cm meatballs. Chill until needed.

To make the soup, heat the stock with the ginger, sugar and fish sauce and leave it to bubble for 5 minutes. Lower in the pork meatballs and gently simmer for 3 minutes (the water should be barely bubbling). Add the cabbage and rice and simmer for a further 2 minutes, or until the meatballs are cooked through.

Divide the soup between 4 bowls, scatter with spring onions and drizzle with sesame oil.

This soup is soothing and restorative, and deliciously delicate, despite its rustic origins. Homemade salt pork makes all the difference to the taste and is very simple to make. You will have to sacrifice some refrigerator space for three days, which is the only complication, but you will be well rewarded.

pork belly & cabbage soup

750 g pork belly, sliced

100 g pickling salt

1 onion, studded with a clove

1 fresh bay leaf

1 cabbage

1 celery stick with leaves, chopped

7 carrots, chopped

4 turnips, chopped

1 tablespoon butter, plus extra for serving

750 g small new potatoes, peeled

salt and black pepper

serves 4–6

Three days before you plan to serve the soup, put the pork belly slices in a shallow ceramic or glass dish and add water to cover. Add the salt and stir until dissolved. Cover and refrigerate for 3 days, turning occasionally. Alternatively, have the butcher salt the pork belly for you.

The day of serving, remove the pork belly from its brine and rinse. Put the pork and onion in a large saucepan with 3 litres water. Bring to the boil and skim off any foam that rises to the surface.

Meanwhile, bring another saucepan of water to the boil with a bay leaf. Add the whole cabbage and blanch for 5 minutes. Remove the cabbage and drain. When cool enough to handle, slice the cabbage.

Add the sliced cabbage, celery, carrots, turnips and butter to the pork. Taste for seasoning. Return to the boil, then lower the heat, cover and simmer for about 30 minutes. Taste for seasoning again.

Add the potatoes and cook until they are tender, 20–25 minutes more. To serve, remove the pork belly and cut into bite-sized pieces. Trim off any rind and discard any bones. Return the pork pieces to the soup and serve hot, with a spoonful of butter in each bowl and thick slices of country bread.

Note If you don't have time to salt the pork yourself, buy a smoked pork knuckle from the butcher and proceed as in the main recipe.

This is a thick and unctuous soup; the kind to be enjoyed in the depths of winter. It's very heavy so a little goes a long way. Serve it as a meal in itself with some bread, rather than as a starter.

parsnip, chorizo & chestnut soup

125 g cooking chorizo, cubed

1 onion, chopped

3 garlic cloves, chopped

1 celery stick, chopped

1 carrot, chopped

3 parsnips, chopped

¼ teaspoon dried chilli flakes

1 teaspoon ground cumin

200 g peeled, cooked chestnuts (fresh or vacuum-packed)

1 litre chicken stock

salt and black pepper

serves 4–6

Put the chorizo in a large saucepan and heat gently for 2–3 minutes until the oil seeps out and the chorizo becomes slightly crispy. Lift out the chorizo with a slotted spoon, trying to leave as much oil behind as you can and set to one side.

Add the onion, garlic, celery, carrot and parsnips to the pan, stir well, cover and cook gently for 10 minutes, or until softening. Add the chilli flakes and cumin, season and stir to release the aroma. Add the chestnuts and stock, then cover and simmer over low heat for 25–30 minutes until everything is very tender.

Transfer the contents of the pan to a blender and liquidize until smooth. Reheat the chorizo in a small frying pan.

Divide the soup between 4–6 bowls and scatter with the crispy chorizo.

This soup is high in flavour and needs no embellishments, making it refreshingly simple to prepare. Make sure you buy the correct chorizo – you want the short, fat, little cured sausages. They are ready to eat but are so much better fried and crispy.

chickpea & chorizo soup

200 g chorizo, roughly chopped

1 red onion, chopped

2 garlic cloves, crushed

400 g canned chopped tomatoes

2 sprigs of fresh thyme

400 g canned chickpeas, rinsed and drained

1 litre vegetable stock

salt and black pepper

serves 4

Put the chorizo in a large saucepan over medium heat and cook until it starts to release its oil. Continue to cook, stirring, for 4–5 minutes until it is lovely and crisp.

Add the onion and garlic and turn the heat right down to allow them to soften in the chorizo's paprika-infused oil. After 6–7 minutes the onion and garlic should be translucent and glossy. Add the tomatoes and thyme and turn the heat back up. Cook for 5 minutes to intensify the flavour, then add the chickpeas and stock. Return to the boil, cover and simmer for 15 minutes.

Remove the thyme. Season well and simmer for a further 10 minutes to allow all the flavours to mingle.

Divide between 4 bowls and serve.

Red lentils have the advantage of cooking quickly into a beautifully coloured purée. They carry other flavours in a most delicious way. Top them with chorizo, the cooking kind.

red lentil & chorizo soup

4 tablespoons olive oil

1 onion, finely chopped

1 carrot, diced

1 celery stick, diced

2 garlic cloves, chopped

3 cm fresh ginger, grated

½ teaspoon smoked sweet Spanish paprika

500 g red lentils

1 litre chicken stock

2–3 chorizo sausages for cooking, finely sliced

2 tablespoons chopped fresh flat leaf parsley

serves 4

Heat 3 tablespoons of the oil in a large saucepan, add the onion, carrot and celery and fry until softened but not browned. Add the garlic and ginger and fry until the garlic has softened but is not browned. Stir in the paprika, then add the lentils and stir to cover. Add the stock. Bring to the boil and simmer until the lentils are tender – they will turn into a purée.

Meanwhile, heat the remaining oil in a frying pan, add the chorizo slices in a single layer and fry until they are lightly browned. Turn them over and lightly fry the other side until crisp. Remove to a plate until ready to serve. Keep the frying oil.

Test the texture of the lentil soup – if too thick, stir in extra boiling stock or water. Ladle into bowls, top with the chorizo and parsley, and spoon the reserved frying oil over the top – it will be a brilliant orange-red.

This deliciously simple soup hails from the south of France. It's substantial enough to serve as a simple winter supper. Any leftovers will reheat well the next day though you're unlikely to have any left!

sausage soup

16 thin pork sausages, pricked with a fork

3 onions, chopped

3 tomatoes, skinned, deseeded and chopped

olive oil

250 g smoked pancetta or streaky bacon, coarsely chopped

2 garlic cloves, crushed with a pinch of salt

a large sprig of fresh sage, sliced

1 baguette, sliced

250 g cheese, such as Cheddar, coarsely grated

salt and black pepper

chopped fresh parsley, to serve (optional)

serves 4

Preheat the oven to 200°C (400°F) Gas 6.

Arrange the sausages in a ring around a large, shallow, flameproof casserole dish. Put the onions and tomatoes in the middle and sprinkle with olive oil. Cook in the preheated oven until done (about 30 minutes, depending on the thickness of the sausages). Stir the onions and tomatoes after 15–20 minutes to stop them burning.

When the sausages are done, cut into 3–4 pieces each and set aside. Put the dish on top of the stove and add the bacon. Fry, stirring, until crisp, and the fat is starting to run. Add the garlic and fry for about 1 minute, then add the sage. Add about 1 litre water and stir. Taste and adjust the seasoning. Add extra water if the mixture is too thick.

Meanwhile, put the slices of baguette on a baking tray and cook at the top of the oven until golden brown. Remove from the oven and sprinkle with grated cheese. Return to the oven until the cheese has melted and become almost crisp.

To serve, put about 3 cheese-topped croutes in 4 soup plates, ladle in the soup and top with the sausages. Sprinkle with parsley, if using, and serve.

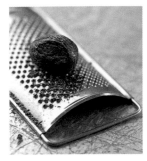

This soup verges on being a casserole. The thick wintry mix of tender lentils with chunks of sausage is so filling, it's perfect to get you ready for a long walk, or maybe just a long snooze on the sofa.

split pea & sausage soup

2 tablespoons olive oil

1 onion, chopped

1 leek, chopped

2 celery sticks, chopped

a pinch of grated nutmeg

300 g yellow split peas

1.5 litres chicken stock

2 dried bay leaves

250 g sausages

salt and black pepper

serves 6

Heat the oil in a large saucepan and cook the onion, leek and celery gently over low heat for 8–10 minutes. Add the nutmeg and stir in. Add the split peas and mix into the vegetables. Add the stock and bay leaves, cover and simmer for 45 minutes or until the peas are tender and beginning to get mushy when pressed with the back of a spoon.

Meanwhile, grill the sausages until cooked, then roughly chop. Add to the soup and cook for a further 10 minutes. Season to taste.

Divide the soup between 6 bowls and serve.

While Tom Yam is well known in Western countries, Tom Som is less so, although it is an equal favourite inside Thailand. The sparerib-based stock includes a mixture of garlic, shallots, ginger and tamarind water – the latter contributing its strong, sour taste. It offers an exciting alternative to the traditional Tom Yam soup.

sparerib & tamarind soup

1 teaspoon black peppercorns

1 tablespoon finely chopped coriander root

2 garlic cloves

4 small shallots

1 tablespoon groundnut or sunflower oil

1.25 litres chicken stock

500 g small pork spareribs, chopped into 2.5-cm pieces

5 cm fresh ginger, finely sliced into matchsticks

2 tablespoons tamarind water

2 tablespoons sugar

3 tablespoons fish sauce

4 spring onions, chopped into 2.5-cm lengths

serves 4

Using a pestle and mortar, pound the peppercorns, coriander root, garlic and shallots to form a paste.

Heat the oil in a large saucepan, add the paste and fry for 5 seconds, stirring well. Add the stock and bring to the boil, stirring well. Add the spareribs and return to the boil.

Add the ginger, tamarind water, sugar, fish sauce and spring onions. Return to the boil again and simmer for 1 minute. Divide between 4 bowls and serve.

Note If you can't find tamarind water, tamarind paste is readily available in supermarkets. For this recipe, mix 1 tablespoon paste with 1 tablespoon water.

fish & seafood

All fishing communities seem to have their version of fish stew or soup. Cioppino is the creation of Italian fishermen in San Francisco and is made with delicious shellfish. If you don't have any Zinfandel to hand, substitute it for another red wine.

cioppino

4 tablespoons olive oil

2 onions, finely chopped

3 red peppers, chopped

6 garlic cloves, crushed

500 ml fish stock

500 ml Zinfandel

500 g canned plum tomatoes

a large sprig of fresh thyme

2 bay leaves

1 teaspoon dried chilli flakes

500 g clams

500 g mussels, cleaned
(see page 200)

12 shelled large raw prawns

500 g scallops

a large bunch of fresh flat leaf
parsley, chopped

salt and black pepper

a handful of basil leaves, to
serve

serves 4

Heat the oil in a large casserole over low heat. Add the onions and peppers and cook slowly for 5 minutes. Add the garlic and continue simmering until the onions have softened, about 15–20 minutes.

Add the stock, wine, tomatoes and their juices, thyme, bay leaves and chilli flakes and bring to the boil over high heat. Reduce the heat and let simmer for about 30 minutes. The soup base can be held at this point until ready to serve. If you want to prepare this part of the soup ahead, cool and refrigerate until next day.

When ready to serve, put about 3 cm water in a large saucepan, add the clams and mussels, in batches if necessary, and bring to the boil with the lid on. Remove them as they open – try not to overcook, or they will be tough. Discard any shells that don't open. Strain the cooking liquid to remove any grit, then add to the soup base.

Bring the soup base to the boil, reduce the heat, add the prawns and scallops and cook for about 1 minute until opaque. Add the reserved clams and mussels, let reheat for about 1 minute, season to taste, then stir in the chopped parsley. Serve topped with the basil leaves.

This is an Italian seafood stew which begs for a big glass of wine and a hunk of ciabatta to accompany it. If you want to bulk out the soup a bit, toast a piece of bread and spoon the soup over it. It's a great way of using up stale bread, which in its soggy state tastes no different to fresh.

cacciucco with gremolata

500 g mussels, cleaned*

2 tablespoons olive oil

1 onion, chopped

2 carrots, diced

2 celery sticks, chopped

4 garlic cloves, sliced

1 red chilli, chopped

400 g canned plum tomatoes

200 ml white wine

2 dried bay leaves

1 litre fish stock

500 g sea bass fillets

6 uncooked tiger prawns

300 g squid, cut into rings

gremolata

zest and juice of 1 lemon

1 tablespoon olive oil

2 garlic cloves, chopped

5 g fresh flat leaf parsley, chopped

serves 4

To make the gremolata, mix together the lemon zest, juice, olive oil, garlic and parsley. Season well and set aside.

Heat the olive oil in a large saucepan and fry the onion, carrots, celery and garlic for 8–10 minutes until softened. Add the chilli, tomatoes, half the white wine, the bay leaves and stock and bring to the boil.

Pour the remaining white wine into another pan and bring to the boil. Add the mussels, cover with a lid and cook over high heat for 3–4 minutes until the shells open. Discard the cooking liquid and transfer the mussels to the soup pan. Discard any mussels that still have not opened. Add the fish and prawns to the pan and simmer gently for 2–3 minutes or until cooked through. Add the squid and cook for 1 minute.

Divide the soup between 4 bowls and spoon over the gremolata.

*Note To prepare mussels, start 15 minutes before you are ready to use. Rinse them in cold water and tap any open ones against the work surface. Discard any that don't close. Scrub the others with a stiff brush. Pull off and discard the wiry beards.

Almost everyone in South-east Asia has a version of this soup. Interestingly it is the tomatoes as well as the obvious tamarind that are seen as the sour part of the soup. You can reduce the heat of the soup by deseeding the chillies.

hot & sour soup

1 litre fish stock

3 lemongrass stalks, halved and crushed

2 red chillies, halved

1 tablespoon tamarind paste

3 tablespoons fish sauce

1 tablespoon sugar

2 small tomatoes, in wedges

500 g fish, such as kingfish, cut crosswise into 4-cm steaks

4–8 shelled medium raw prawns

a handful of beansprouts

2 spring onions, chopped

to serve

2 limes, halved

a small dish of fish sauce

a small dish of chopped chillies

4 large handfuls of fresh herbs, such as coriander and mint

serves 4

Put the stock in a large saucepan, add the lemongrass, chillies, tamarind paste, fish sauce and sugar. Bring to the boil and simmer for about 5 minutes. Add the tomatoes. Taste and adjust the seasoning with more fish sauce or sugar, as you like.

Add the fish and simmer for a few minutes until the flesh is opaque. Add the prawns and simmer until they are opaque and pink at the edges. Don't overcook or you will lose the flavour.

Put the beansprouts and spring onions into soup bowls, add the fish and prawns and handfuls of herbs. Ladle the broth over the top. Serve with little dishes of limes, fish sauce, chillies and more herbs.

Variation To make a more substantial meal, prepare your choice of rice noodles and add to the bowls before the beansprouts.

This soup can be made successfully without hard-to-come-by Mediterranean fish and is quick to make. The bones and prawn shells add flavour, as well as making it a bit messy, but this is fishermen's fare, so roll up your sleeves and enjoy.

Basque fish soup

2 tablespoons olive oil

1 red pepper, sliced

1 onion, sliced

3 garlic cloves, crushed

1 green chilli, chopped

¼ teaspoon hot paprika

a sprig of fresh thyme

225 g canned chopped tomatoes

1.5 litres fish stock

250 g monkfish fillet, cut into bite-sized pieces

500 g hake or cod steaks

250 g unpeeled prawn tails

250 ml dry white wine

500 g fresh mussels (see page 200)

a handful of chopped fresh flat leaf parsley

serves 4–6

Heat the oil in a large saucepan. Add the pepper and onion and cook until browned, about 5 minutes. Stir in the garlic, chilli, paprika, thyme and tomatoes and cook for 5 minutes more.

Add the stock, monkfish, hake and prawns. Bring to the boil, skim off the foam and simmer until the fish is cooked through, 10–15 minutes.

Pour the wine into a large saucepan with a lid and bring to the boil for 1 minute, then remove from the heat. Add the prepared mussels to the wine, cover and steam over high heat just until opened, 2–3 minutes. Remove the mussels from their shells, discarding any that do not open.

Add the mussels and cooking liquid to the soup and stir well. Sprinkle with parsley and serve immediately, with baguette on the side.

This soup is packed with the flavours of the Mediterranean. Enjoy it with a glass of white wine and some toasted baguette – it will taste as good as it would on a seaside terrace.

Mediterranean fish soup

3 kg fish and seafood, such as red snapper, bream, monkfish, sea bass, squid, clams and crayfish or large prawn tails

20 black peppercorns

a large bunch of mixed fresh herbs, such as parsley, rosemary and marjoram

300 ml dry white wine

300 ml fish stock or water

2 tablespoons extra virgin olive oil

1 large red onion, sliced

4 garlic cloves, sliced

2 dried red chillies, crushed

4 plum tomatoes, skinned or 450 g canned chopped tomatoes

4–6 slices of bread, 2 cm thick, toasted

serves 4–6

Chop the fish into 5-cm chunks or, if small, leave whole. Put in a large, flameproof casserole. Add the peppercorns, herbs, wine and stock. Bring to the boil, then reduce the heat to a gentle simmer and cover. Cook for 5–6 minutes.

Using a slotted spoon, remove the fish to a plate and keep hot. Measure the broth – there should be about 550 ml or so – if not add extra water. Pour into a jug or bowl.

Add the oil, onion, garlic and chillies to the hot pan, fry for 2 minutes, then add the tomatoes. Return the fish and broth to the pan. Bring back to simmering and serve ladled over chunks of toasted bread as soup, then ladle out the fish as a stew. Alternatively, serve both at the same time.

This superb, ancient recipe from Provence excites huge passion. Bouillabaisse consists of fragrant fish chunks poached in a saffron-enhanced broth, with aromatics. The dish is served as two courses: first the broth is spooned over toasted bread croutes topped with *rouille* sauce, which enriches the soup; next the fish itself is eaten.

French bouillabaisse

50 ml extra virgin olive oil

2 onions, quartered

2 leeks, cut in 5-cm chunks

4 garlic cloves, chopped

2 large tomatoes, quartered

a bunch of fresh thyme, about 50 g

1 fennel bulb, quartered

20-cm strip of orange zest

1 kg mixed fish fillets, in 4-cm chunks

1 kg mixed shellfish

a large pinch of saffron threads

250 ml garlic mayonnaise

500 g new potatoes, boiled

4 tablespoons harissa paste

salt and black pepper

1 baguette, sliced and toasted, to serve

serves 4–6

Heat half the oil in a large, flameproof casserole, add the onions, leeks, garlic and tomatoes and fry until golden and wilted. Add the thyme, fennel and orange zest. Add 2 litres boiling water and the remaining oil, then the fish, shellfish and half the saffron.

Return to the boil, reduce the heat and simmer for 10–12 minutes.

Pour the pan contents through a colander into a large bowl. Lift out the fish into a large, heated tureen or serving dish. Using a slotted spoon, press down on the onions, fennel, thyme and tomatoes in the colander, then discard them.

Pour the broth back into the pan, bring to the boil and cook over very high heat for 5 minutes until emulsified, then whisk in half the garlic mayonnaise. Add the potatoes. Pour about a quarter of the mixture over the fish.

Put a slice of baguette on the side of each bowl, then add a generous spoonful of garlic mayonnaise to each. Mix the remaining mayonnaise with the harissa and remaining saffron to create a scarlet rouille sauce. Add a spoonful of rouille to the croutes. Ladle hot soup into each dish. When the soup is finished, serve the fish and hot potatoes with any remaining garlic mayonnaise and rouille.

This dish is all about the quality of the produce. The soup base can be made a few hours in advance, up to the point where you've added and cooked the rice. All you need to do is reheat the soup and add the fresh seafood when you are ready to serve it to your guests.

Spanish bouillabaisse

2 tablespoons olive oil

1 red onion, chopped

2 garlic cloves, chopped

1 chorizo sausage, finely chopped

1 carrot, grated

1 teaspoon grated orange zest

2 litres fish stock

400 g canned chopped tomatoes

55 g arborio (risotto) rice

200 g skinless salmon fillet, cut into 2-cm pieces

1 cleaned squid tube, thinly sliced

12 raw prawns, peeled and deveined

a handful of chopped fresh flat leaf parsley leaves

salt and black pepper

serves 4

Heat the oil in a large saucepan set over medium heat. Add the onion, garlic, chorizo, carrot and orange zest and cook for about 10 minutes, stirring often, until softened and aromatic. Add the fish stock, tomatoes and rice and bring to the boil. Reduce the heat to medium and let simmer, uncovered, for about 15 minutes, until the soup thickens and the rice is cooked.

Add the prepared salmon, squid and prawns, cover and cook for 2–3 minutes, until the seafood is all cooked through and the prawns are pink. Season to taste with salt and pepper and stir in the parsley. Ladle into serving bowls and serve immediately.

Smoked haddock provides that warm smoky flavour that cold wintry nights call for. Beans work well in soups – they are quick and easy to throw in and thicken up soups nicely. Cannellini and butter beans have been used in this recipe but can be substituted if you wish.

smoked haddock & bean soup

4 tablespoons olive oil

1 red onion, sliced

600 ml fish stock

3 dried bay leaves

finely grated zest of
1 unwaxed lemon

300 g smoked haddock,
skinned and cubed

400 g canned cannellini beans,
rinsed and drained

400 g canned butter beans,
rinsed and drained

4 tablespoons crème fraîche

salt and black pepper

serves 4

Heat the oil in a large saucepan, then fry the onion. Cover and cook over low heat for 10 minutes, stirring occasionally until soft.

Pour in the stock, add the bay leaves and lemon zest and bring to a gentle simmer. Add the smoked haddock and cook for 3–4 minutes until opaque. It will continue to cook in the residual heat too.

Liquidize half the cannellini and half the butter beans with 200 ml water in a blender and stir into the soup. Stir in the remaining whole beans and the crème fraîche. Season with salt. If the soup is too thick, add some water to thin it down.

Divide the soup between 4 bowls and serve with a fresh grinding of black pepper.

This chunky soup is full of interesting flavours. Lentils not only give the soup colour and texture, they pack a powerful protein punch, while also helping to maintain a healthy digestive system and reducing cholesterol.

smoked haddock & Puy lentil chowder

100 g Puy lentils, rinsed

2 leeks, chopped

600 ml vegetable, fish or chicken stock

8 small new potatoes, scrubbed and diced

300 ml skimmed milk

350 g smoked haddock fillets, skinned

2 tablespoons finely snipped fresh chives

salt and black pepper

serves 4

Put the rinsed lentils in a saucepan, add enough boiling water to cover the lentils by 4 cm, cover the saucepan and simmer for 15–20 minutes until tender, then drain.

Meanwhile, simmer the leeks in 4 tablespoons of the stock in a large saucepan, covered, for 3–4 minutes until softened. Stir in the potatoes, milk and remaining stock. Season and bring to the boil, then simmer for 15 minutes or until the potatoes are tender.

Add the smoked haddock to the saucepan and simmer for 4–5 minutes until the fish flakes easily. Lift the haddock out of the pan and break into large flakes.

Stir the lentils into the chowder, ladle into bowls and top with the flaked smoked haddock. Add a scattering of chives and serve.

Japanese broths always feel like they are doing you the world of good. If you can't get hold of kombu (a Japanese seaweed sold dried in packets) and bonito flakes, you could use a fish stock mixed with miso soup. If you're short on time or wish to cut down on ingredients you can always opt for shop-bought teriyaki sauce.

teriyaki mackerel & noodle soup

200 g shiitake mushrooms, sliced

200 g udon noodles

100 g baby spinach leaves

1 tablespoon light soy sauce

6 spring onions, shredded and left in iced water to curl

teriyaki mackerel

3 tablespoons light soy sauce

2 tablespoons sake

2 teaspoons sugar

½ teaspoon freshly grated ginger

4 mackerel fillets

ginger dashi

15 cm kombu or
1 tablespoon instant dashi with bonito flakes

5 cm fresh ginger, thinly sliced

serves 4

To make the teriyaki, mix the soy sauce, sake, sugar and ginger together in a shallow dish. Add the fish, toss well to coat in the teriyaki and marinate for 15 minutes while you make the dashi.

To make the dashi, put the kombu and 1 litre water in a saucepan and gently heat, skimming off any scum. Just before it boils, remove and discard the kombu. Add the ginger to the water, bring to the boil, then strain though a fine sieve into a large saucepan. Alternatively, make up 800 ml instant dashi in a large saucepan. Add the shiitake mushrooms to the homemade or instant dashi and cook for 5 minutes or until softening.

Preheat the grill.

Cook the noodles in a pan of water according to the manufacturer's instructions, drain and run under cold water. Put the marinated fish on a baking tray and grill for 3 minutes on each side until cooked through. Add the spinach to the dashi, along with the noodles.

Divide the soup between 4 bowls, season with soy sauce, top with a piece of fish and scatter with the spring onions.

A bourride is a little like a bouillabaisse but thickened with a garlicky aïoli. This soup works well for dinner parties, as it looks like you really know what you're doing and the toast, cheese and aïoli get people involved and thinking about what they are eating.

monkfish, fennel & saffron bourride

3 tablespoons olive oil

1 onion, chopped

1 fennel bulb, finely chopped

1 leek, white part sliced

300 g new potatoes, sliced

¼ teaspoon saffron threads

2 fresh sprigs of thyme

2 large tomatoes, thinly sliced

600 g monkfish fillets, sliced

1 litre fish stock

salt and black pepper

Gruyère cheese, grated, to serve

aïoli

2 egg yolks

1 teaspoon Dijon mustard

200 ml olive oil

2 garlic cloves, crushed

2 teaspoons harissa

1 tablespoon lemon juice

serves 4–6

Heat the oil in a large saucepan and fry the onion, fennel and leek over low heat for 5 minutes. Add the potatoes, saffron and thyme, stirring once or twice. Cook until the potato starts to soften.

Add the tomatoes and monkfish in a layer on top and, without stirring, pour in the stock. It should come at least halfway up the fish; if not, top up with water. Bring to the boil over gentle heat with the lid on and cook for 10–12 minutes until the fish is cooked and the potatoes are tender.

Meanwhile, to make the aïoli, put the egg yolks and mustard in a medium mixing bowl and whisk with electric beaters. Trickle in the olive oil slowly, whisking until it emulsifies and thickens. Season then stir in the garlic, harissa and lemon juice. Transfer half the aïoli to a serving dish.

Siphon off 2–3 ladlefuls of the liquid in the saucepan, add it to the remaining aïoli and stir well until combined. Stir back into the saucepan. Warm over low heat and season to taste, but don't boil.

Divide the soup between 4–6 bowls and serve with toast, extra aïoli and Gruyère.

This elegant dinner dish can be on the table in about 8 minutes –
30 if you're chatting and enjoying yourself over a glass of wine.
Add whatever vegetables you have on hand.

grilled salmon noodle soup

1 tub silken tofu

2 bundles soba noodles

4 large salmon steaks, skin on

2 tablespoons sunflower oil

1 litre dashi stock

your choice of other vegetables,
such as sugar snap peas
(a large handful per serving)

a handful of Chinese dried
mushrooms (optional), soaked
in hot water for 20 minutes

about 6 spring onions, sliced,
to serve

fish sauce or soy sauce, to taste
(optional)

freshly sliced chillies or chilli
sauce (optional)

serves 4

To prepare the tofu, put it between 2 plates and put a weight on top (a small can of tuna, for instance). This will force out some of the liquid and make it stick together better. Just before serving, cut into about 12 cubes – 3 cuts one way, 4 the other.

Bring a saucepan of water to the boil and add the noodles. Have a glass of cold water ready. When the water comes to the boil, add a dash of cold water. When it returns to the boil, do it again, return to the boil and do it again. This will help cook the noodles perfectly – the cold water 'scares' the heat into the interior. Test after 3–4 minutes, then drain and keep in cold water until ready to serve.

Put the salmon in a plastic bag, add the oil and toss to coat. Bring a stove-top grill pan or frying pan to a high heat, then add the salmon, skin side down. When the skin is charred and the flesh has turned pale about 1 cm through, turn the salmon over and lightly sear the other side. It should stay pink except for a line on either side.

Bring the dashi to the boil, then lightly blanch your chosen vegetable. Remove with a slotted spoon. Drain the mushrooms and slice into pieces, discarding the hard stalk tip.

Put a pile of drained noodles into each bowl. Put the salmon steaks, skin side up, on top. Add the tofu cubes, mushrooms, if using, and any other vegetables used. Ladle the stock over the top and serve topped with spring onions. If you prefer, add seasoning in the form of salt, soy or fish sauce and fire in the form of fresh chillies or chilli sauce.

There are many kinds of chowder: this New England variety, made with clams and cream; the Manhattan kind, made with tomatoes, and the British kind, made with corn and smoked haddock.

clam chowder

2 kg clams, in the shell

125 ml fish stock or clam juice, plus extra fish stock to make 1 litre

500 g smoked pancetta, cubed

sunflower oil

3 onions, coarsely chopped

1 celery stick, chopped

1 carrot, chopped

2 bay leaves

a few sprigs of fresh thyme

250 g salad potatoes, peeled and cut into dice

500 ml double cream

salt and black pepper

a large bunch of fresh chopped flat leaf parsley

serves 4

Put the clams in a large saucepan, then add 125 ml water and the fish stock or clam juice. Cover the pan, bring to the boil and boil hard until the clams open. Remove them as soon as they do and shell over a bowl. Don't overcook or they will be tough. Discard the shells, reserve the clams and return the juice in the bowl to the pan. Strain the cooking liquid through a sieve, then through muslin into a measuring jug. Add enough fish stock to make up to 1 litre. Taste it and reserve.

Clean the pan, add the pancetta and cook slowly to render the fat (add a dash of oil to encourage it if you like – but sunflower, not olive). Remove the pancetta and set aside.

Add the onions, celery, carrot, bay leaves and thyme to the saucepan. Cook gently until the onions are softened and translucent. Add the potato cubes and the reserved 1 litre stock. Simmer until the potatoes are done, about 10 minutes.

Chop half the clams, and cut the others in half through their thickness. Add the clams, pancetta and cream to the saucepan and heat through. Taste and add salt if necessary. Remove and discard the bay leaves and thyme.

Divide between 4 soup bowls and top with a fresh grinding of pepper.

This soup is a very easy bisque to make. If you want to make your fish stock more shellfishy, you could add some prawn shells to the stock as well as the crab shells. The prawns can be used in a sandwich the next day or even stirred into the bisque at the end. Whole cooked crab is more expensive than crabmeat but worth it.

crab bisque

600 g cooked whole crab

1.25 litres fish stock

150 ml white wine

50 g butter

3 leeks, sliced

300 g potatoes, peeled and diced

1 teaspoon tomato purée

3 tablespoons brandy

2 sprigs of fresh tarragon

3 tablespoons double cream

¼ teaspoon ground mace

juice of ½ lemon

sea salt

a pinch of cayenne pepper, to serve

serves 4

Prise out the white and brown crabmeat from its shell, place in a small bowl and reserve. You should have at least 250 g meat. Put the shell, stock and wine in a saucepan and simmer for 20 minutes.

Heat the butter in a large frying pan over low heat, then add the leeks. Cover and cook for 5 minutes until softened, but not browned. Add the potatoes and give it a good stir, then put the lid back on and cook for a further 5 minutes, giving it a stir every now and then to stop it from sticking. Add the tomato purée, brandy and tarragon and turn up the heat to burn off the alcohol. Once it has evaporated, strain in half the stock mixture and simmer until the potatoes are completely soft, about 15 minutes.

Transfer the contents of the frying pan to a blender and liquidize until smooth. Return to the pan, strain in the remaining stock, then add the reserved crabmeat and the cream. Heat through and season to taste with salt, mace and lemon juice.

Divide the soup between 4 bowls and sprinkle with cayenne pepper.

Lobster bisque is a classic that has withstood the tests of time. Obviously it's not cheap to make, so save it for a special occasion shared with a special someone.

lobster bisque

1 packet Chinese dried shrimp, about 50 g

a large pinch of saffron threads (optional)

2 tablespoons olive oil

2 large shallots, chopped

2 garlic cloves, crushed

at least 500 g cooked lobster shells, well broken

1 litre fish stock

1 fresh bay leaf

2 tablespoons harissa paste

500 g boneless white fish fillets, such as cod

juice of ½ lemon

salt and black pepper

to serve (optional)

toasted baguette

garlic mayonnaise

125 g Gruyère cheese, grated

serves 4

Put the dried shrimp and saffron threads, if using, in a small bowl and cover with boiling water. Set aside until the shrimp soften, about 20 minutes.

Heat the oil in a large, heavy-based saucepan, add the shallots and fry until softened and translucent. Add the garlic and seafood shells and stir-fry until aromatic. Add the stock, bay leaf, dried shrimp and saffron and their soaking liquid. Boil hard for about 5 minutes so the stock and oil amalgamate. Add the harissa and fish and poach for 5 minutes until the fish is opaque.

Remove the bay leaf, strain the soup into a bowl or jug and transfer the solids, including the shells, to a food processor. This is hard labour for the blades, so work in batches and use the metal ones. Add 1–2 ladles of stock and blend until smooth. Push the mixture through a strainer into the rinsed saucepan, then transfer the solids back into the blender. Add more stock, blend again and push through a strainer again. Repeat until all the stock has been used. The more you blend and push, the stronger the flavour will be.

Discard the solids in the strainer and reheat the soup in the saucepan. Stir in the lemon juice and season to taste. Divide between 4 bowls and serve topped with toasted baguette smothered in garlic mayonnaise and Gruyère cheese, if you wish.

This soup has a delicate balance of spicy, fresh, zesty flavours. Buy a bag of kaffir lime leaves and freeze them, then use straight from frozen. Ginger can also be frozen, then grated from frozen. Both flavours contrast well with the richness of coconut milk and lobster.

Thai lobster noodle soup

2 small cooked lobsters or crayfish tails, shells removed

120 g dried shrimp

3 kaffir lime leaves, torn

3 cm fresh ginger, peeled

200 g wide rice noodles

2 tablespoons hijiki seaweed

2 tablespoons mirin

200 ml coconut cream

2 tablespoons fish sauce

juice of 1 lime

2 red chillies, halved lengthways and thinly sliced

2 mild green chillies, deseeded and thinly sliced

a handful of fresh garlic chives, sliced diagonally

75 g thin green beans, sliced in half lengthways and cooked

2 sprigs of fresh Thai sweet basil (optional)

serves 4

Put the lobster shells, dried shrimp and kaffir lime leaves in a large saucepan. Add 1.5 litres water and bring to the boil, then lower the heat and simmer for 1 hour. Strain the stock, grate the ginger and squeeze the juice from it into the stock.

Soak the noodles in a bowl of cold water for 20 minutes. When soft, drain well and cover until needed. Put the seaweed in a bowl and stir in the mirin.

Add the coconut cream to the stock, stir well and bring to the boil. Lower the heat, then add fish sauce and lime juice to taste.

When ready to serve, add the drained noodles to the stock and reheat. Ladle into hot bowls, then add the chillies, chives, beans and lobster meat. Drain the seaweed and sprinkle it over the soup, then top with Thai sweet basil leaves, if using, and serve.

Note Fishmongers and Chinese supermarkets often have frozen crayfish tails, which are good for this recipe. Instead of hijiki seaweed, you can use black sesame seeds to sprinkle on top.

This chilled soup makes an excellent starter for a summer dinner party. Your guests are sure to be impressed by the combination of different flavours and textures.

chilled coconut soup with sizzling prawns

500 ml coconut milk

300 ml plain yoghurt

1 cucumber, peeled and chopped

2 tablespoons chopped fresh mint

2 tablespoons extra virgin olive oil

2 garlic cloves, thinly sliced

½ teaspoon cumin seeds

a pinch of dried chilli flakes

8–12 uncooked tiger prawns, peeled and deveined

salt and black pepper

serves 4

Put the coconut milk, yoghurt, cucumber and mint into a blender and process to a purée. Season to taste and refrigerate for 1 hour.

Ladle the soup into 4 bowls just before starting to cook the prawns.

Put the oil into a large frying pan and heat gently. Add the garlic, cumin seeds and chilli flakes and fry very gently until the garlic is softened, but not golden. Using a slotted spoon, transfer the garlic to a small plate.

Increase the heat and add the prawns to the pan. Stir-fry for about 3–4 minutes until cooked through. Return the garlic mixture to the pan, stir quickly, then immediately spoon the sizzling hot prawns onto the soup and serve.

This is a wonderful meal-in-a-bowl that takes only minutes to put together. It is quite spicy, so reduce the quantity of chilli if you prefer. Tom yum paste is a treasure to have in your storecupboard – it can be used to make stir-fries or Thai curries.

tom yum prawn noodle soup

100 g uncooked large or king prawns, shells on

2 tablespoons tom yum paste

1 red chilli, deseeded and finely chopped

1 red pepper, deseeded and thinly sliced

100 g brown cap mushrooms, sliced

100 g leeks, trimmed and finely diced

100 g rice noodles

to serve

a few sprigs of fresh coriander

juice of 1 lime

serves 2–4

Peel the prawns and use a very sharp knife to cut each one along the back so that it opens out like a butterfly (leaving each prawn joined along the base and at the tail). Remove the black vein.

Bring 570 ml water to the boil in a large pan. Stir in the tom yum paste until dissolved. Add the chilli, red pepper, mushrooms and leeks and let the mixture simmer for 5 minutes.

Meanwhile, put the noodles in a large heatproof bowl, cover with boiling water and leave to sit for 3–5 minutes until just tender before draining in a colander and spooning into deep serving bowls.

Add the prawns to the tom yum mixture and simmer for a further 2–3 minutes. Pour the tom yum soup over the noodles. Squeeze a little lime juice over each bowl and garnish with a coriander sprig. Serve immediately.

This soup never ceases to satisfy and just goes to show that flavour doesn't need to come from butter or cream. The end result is based on a good backbone of flavour which comes from the stock.

prawn tom yam

1 litre chicken stock

1 lemongrass stalk, halved lengthways and bruised

3 cm fresh ginger, thinly sliced

3 kaffir lime leaves

a small handful of fresh coriander, stalks finely chopped and leaves left whole

2 shallots, sliced

3 chillies, deseeded and shredded

150 g button mushrooms, halved

200 g uncooked king prawns, deveined and shelled but tails left intact

80 ml lime juice

2 tablespoons sugar

4 tablespoons fish sauce

serves 4–6

Put the stock in a large saucepan with the lemongrass, ginger, lime leaves, chopped coriander stalks, shallots, chillies and mushrooms. Bring to the boil, turn down the heat and simmer for 10 minutes.

Butterfly the prawns (cut down the back lengthways with a sharp knife) and add them to the pan with the lime juice, sugar and fish sauce and simmer for 1 minute or until the prawns are pink. Scatter the reserved coriander leaves into the soup. Take off the heat and taste, adding more fish sauce, lime juice or sugar, as you see fit.

Divide the soup between 4–6 bowls and serve.

index

recipe credits

Fiona Beckett
Fennel, leek & cauliflower soup

Vatcharin Bhumichitr
Cauliflower & coconut soup
Sparerib & tamarind soup

Celia Brooks Brown
Celeriac & orange soup
Lentil, coconut & spinach soup

Maxine Clark
Cream of chickpea soup with wild mushrooms
Fiery red pepper soup
La ribollita
Leek & potato soup
Pasta & bean soup
Spinach broth with egg & cheese
Tuscan bean soup with rosemary

Ross Dobson
Carrot & lentil soup
Chickpea, tomato & green bean minestrone
Chunky chickpea soup
Creamy cauliflower & Gruyère soup
Fresh sweetcorn & chicken soup
Garlic & chilli rice soup with spring greens
Globe artichoke, tarragon & Roquefort soup
Peppery watercress & pea soup with Gorgonzola
Roasted tomato soup with rarebit toasts
Scotch broth
Summer sweetcorn soup
Sweet potato & coconut soup with Thai pesto
Swiss chard & white bean minestrone

Clare Ferguson
Bouillabaisse
Mediterranean fish soup

Silvana Franco
Conchigliette soup
Summer minestrone

Liz Franklin
Ajo blanco

Manisha Gambir Harkins
Andalusian chickpea soup
Butternut squash soup with allspice & pine nuts
Cajun-spiced chowder with corn & bacon

Tonia George
Beef, tamarind & sweet potato soup
Cacciucco with gremolata
Cauliflower & Stilton soup
Chicken avgolemono
Chickpea, tomato & chorizo soup
Chilled avocado soup with coriander
Chunky Puy lentil & vegetable soup
Courgette, broad bean & lemon broth
Crab bisque
French onion soup
Gazpacho
Harrira
Lentil, spinach & cumin soup
Minestrone with Parmesan rind
Minty pea risotto soup
Monkfish, fennel & saffron bourride
Mushroom soup with Madeira & hazelnuts
Parsnip, chorizo & chestnut soup
Potato, bacon & Savoy cabbage soup
Prawn tom yam
Roast aubergine, red pepper & oregano soup
Roast chicken, garlic & watercress soup
Rocket soup with poached egg & truffle oil
Smoked haddock & bean soup

Spiced carrot soup
Spiced pumpkin &coconut soup
Split pea & sausage soup
Sweetcorn & pancetta chowder
Teriyaki mackerel & shiitake noodle soup
Thai chicken, mushroom & coconut soup
Thai pork & rice soup
Tomato, chilli & rosemary soup
Turkish leek, barley & yoghurt soup
Vietnamese beef pho

Rachael Anne Hill
Full of beans soup

Rachael Anne Hill & Tamsin Burnett-Hall
Chickpea, lemon & mint soup
Smoked haddock & Puy lentil chowder

Jennifer Joyce
Chicken noodle soup

Caroline Marson
Chicken, lemongrass, ginger & rice soup
Spiced butternut squash & coconut soup
Tom yum prawn noodle soup

Elsa Petersen-Schepelern
Alphabet soup
Avgolemono
Bisque
Carrot vichyssoise
Chicken soup with vegetables
Cioppino
Clam chowder
Cream of broccoli soup with leeks & broad beans
Cream of mushroom soup
Duck soup
Flag bean soup

Goan chicken soup
Hot & sour soup
Iced beetroot soup
Indonesian chicken noodle soup
Japanese fresh corn soup
Laksa
Minestra di farro
Red lentil & chorizo soup
Salmon noodle soup
Sausage soup
Swedish yellow pea
Tomato & pesto soup
Wonton chicken soup

Louise Pickford
Chilled coconut soup with sizzling prawns
Chilled melon soup with Serrano ham

Linda Tubby
Herb & carrot soup
Soupe verdon
Thai lobster noodle soup

Laura Washburn
Cabbage soup
Courgette, corn & cumin soup
Green vegetable soup
Lentil soup with roasted Tomatoes & onions
Soupe au pistou
Vegetable bouillabaisse

photography credits

Key: a=above, b=below, r=right, l=left, c=centre.

Henry Bourne
Page 182

Martin Brigdale
Pages 25, 26, 30, 32, 33, 48, 85, 111, 116, 160, 161, 183, 185, 205, 206, 209

Peter Cassidy
Pages 3r, 7, 10, 14, 18, 24, 28, 29, 38, 41, 42, 45, 49, 52, 53, 62, 67, 70, 76, 87, 89, 97, 103, 108, 112, 115, 135, 146, 148, 152, 154, 156, 157, 162, 165, 168, 171, 176, 177, 188, 191, 193, 195, 198, 202, 221, 222, 226, 229, 233

Nicki Dowey
Page 104

Tara Fisher
Page 83

Richard Jung
Pages 3l, 11, 15, 19, 34, 40, 50, 86, 90, 93, 94, 95, 101, 106, 107, 120, 123, 124, 150, 164, 167

Lisa Linder
Pages 56, 143

William Lingwood
Pages 17, 22, 60

Diana Miller
Pages 36, 99, 173

Noel Murphy
Pages 66, 81

David Munns
Pages 61, 131

William Reavell
Pages 1, 73, 77, 119, 127, 187, 214

Yuki Sugiura
Page 2, 3cl, 3cr, 4, 5, 6, 8, 9, 13, 21, 37, 46, 54, 58, 65, 69, 74, 78, 82, 98, 102, 132, 136, 137, 140, 141, 142, 145, 149, 153, 158, 172, 175, 179, 180, 184, 192, 196, 197, 201, 213, 217, 218, 225, 234, 240

Ian Wallace
Pages 138, 230

Philip Webb
Pages 57, 128

Kate Whitaker
Pages 169, 210

Francesca Yorke
Page 72